AIR CAMPAIGN

# BLOODY APRIL 1917

The birth of modern air power

JAMES S. CORUM | ILLUSTRATED BY GRAHAM TURNER

OSPREY PUBLISHING
Bloomsbury Publishing Plc
Kemp House, Chawley Park, Cumnor Hill, Oxford OX2 9PH, UK
29 Earlsfort Terrace, Dublin 2, Ireland
1385 Broadway, 5th Floor, New York, NY 10018, USA
E-mail: info@ospreypublishing.com
www.ospreypublishing.com

OSPREY is a trademark of Osprey Publishing Ltd

First published in Great Britain in 2022

A catalogue record for this book is available from the British Library.

ISBN: PB 9781472853059; eBook 9781472853042;
ePDF 9781472853066; XML 9781472853073

22 23 24 25 26 10 9 8 7 6 5 4 3 2 1

Maps by www.bounford.com
Diagrams by Adam Tooby
3D BEVs by Paul Kime
Index by Alan Rutter
Typeset by PDQ Digital Media Solutions, Bungay, UK
Printed and bound in India by Replika Press Private Ltd.

Osprey Publishing supports the Woodland Trust, the UK's leading woodland
conservation charity.

To find out more about our authors and books visit www.ospreypublishing.com. Here
you will find extracts, author interviews, details of forthcoming events and the option to
sign up for our newsletter.

## GLOSSARY

### Organizations
**German:**
*Oberste Heeresleitung*: Supreme
High Command
*Luftstreitkräfte*: German Imperial
Air Service
*Flieger Abteilung*: Flight Detachment
(flight of six artillery or observa-
tion planes)
*Jagdstaffel* (*Jasta*): Fighter Squadron
(12 planes)
*Jagdgeschwader* (*JG*): Fighter Wing
(three to four Jastas)
*Schutzstaffel* (*Schusta*): Protection
Squadron (six two-seater escorts)
*Schlachtstaffel* (*Schlasta*): Battle Squadron
(six ground-attack aircraft)
*Schlachtgruppe*: Ground-Attack Group
(three *Schlachtstaffel*)
*Luftschutzoffizier*: Air Defence Officer
(commander observation post on the
front lines)

**French:**
*Service Aéronautique*: French Army
Air Service
*Escadrille*: Squadron (ten planes)
*Escadre*: Wing (three or four *Escadrilles*)
*Groupe de Combat*: Group (three or four
fighter *Escadrilles*)

**British:**
BEF: British Expeditionary Force
RFC: Royal Flying Corps
RNAS: Royal Naval Air Service

### Ranks:
*Commandant* (Fr): Major
*Hauptmann* (Ger): Captain
*Rittmeister* (Ger): Captain
*Freiherr* (Ger): Baron

### Places:
*Siegfriedstellung*: Hindenburg Line

### Aircraft designations
**German:**
D aircraft: single seat fighters
C aircraft: two-seat observation/
artillery aircraft
CL aircraft: two-seat ground-attack
aircraft
G aircraft: two-engine heavy bombers

**French:**
French squadrons named after the main
aircraft type of the unit
C: Caudron, N: Nieuport, F: Farman, V:
Voisin, Spa: SPAD etc.

**British:**
pusher biplanes: aircraft with the engine
and propeller located to the rear behind
the pilot

# CONTENTS

# INTRODUCTION

The Allied offensive of April 1917, known as the Nivelle Offensive, brought an entirely new level of operational airpower to the World War I battlefields. The previous year had seen the first true air campaigns at Verdun and the Somme, in which bombers, reconnaissance aircraft and fighters all supported the operational plan. Yet those air campaigns were relatively primitive in operational control, organization and tactics compared to the more complex air campaigns waged in April 1917 by the British in the Arras sector and the French at Chemin des Dames. The Germans also developed new organizations and operational doctrine for their defensive campaign.

The air campaign of spring 1917 saw significant changes in the use of airpower, to the extent that the period represents a major evolutionary step forward. While most books and articles about the World War I air war focus on the exploits of the fighter aces, it must be noted that fighters were only one factor in the use of operational airpower, and not even the most important. In terms of military strategy and operations, the celebrated aces performed a subordinate role and were not the main mission for air operations. This book will focus on Allied and German airpower at the operational level in spring 1917 – it was at this level that fundamental changes in doctrine, tactics and organization were made – and how this affected the outcome of the war.

For the Allied and the German senior commanders in 1917, the main role of airpower was to support the ground armies. In particular, this meant that airpower's primary mission was to support the artillery. Without constant aerial reconnaissance, and without the efforts of the radio-equipped artillery observation squadrons of the Allies and the Germans, the primary weapon of World War I armies – artillery – could not be used effectively. Two-seater reconnaissance and observation aircraft constituted most of the Royal Flying Corps, the German *Luftstreitkräfte* and the French *Service Aéronautique* in 1917. The fighter squadrons fought to gain air superiority over the front to allow the reconnaissance and artillery flyers of both sides to conduct their essential missions.

Spring of 1917 prompted major changes for the aviation forces in organization, command and control, and in operational, defensive and offensive air doctrine. The spring 1917 campaign also saw major changes in the equipment and tactics of aviation forces. By early 1917, the three air services were vastly different from the year before. In October 1916, the Germans had reorganized their air service into the Luftstreitkräfte, which was given responsibility and command of all German aviation forces, including balloons, anti-aircraft guns, home and training units as well as front-line units. The Luftstreitkräfte had its own General Staff and commanded all aviation, serving as a modern air force with its own commander and operating, like the army, under the direction of Germany's Supreme High Command (*Oberste Heeresleitung*).

In 1917, the Luftstreitkräfte organized its front aviation units into groups, squadrons and flights, with most units assigned to one of Germany's 19 armies in the field. Each army had an army aviation commander. Due to this rapid expansion of units in the winter of 1916–17, the Luftstreitkräfte created the position of Group Commander. The Group Commander, with his staff, commanded reconnaissance, artillery and escort squadrons (called *Schutzstaffel*) for a sector of the front aligned to support one of the army's corps. The Luftstreitkräfte had created its own signals service to ensure army aviation and group commanders were fully tied to the army units they supported. The French Service Aéronautique underwent changes after the Verdun battles. In late 1916, the squadron size was expanded to ten aircraft, and squadrons were now normally organized into combat groups of three or four squadrons, under a group commander. In early 1917, the French also created the position of air commander for each army group, who would oversee the plans and operations of the army aviation commanders. The British Royal Flying Corps was rapidly expanding. RFC wings, a group of three or more squadrons, were organized into air brigades, with command headquarters for two or more wings. A RFC brigade served as the aviation command and control element for each of the British field armies.

Air doctrine early in the war mostly consisted of short memos and directives, but 1917 saw air services publishing extensive manuals at the operational level, specifying how a large number of squadrons and groups would coordinate their efforts to support the campaign plan. The campaign plans of all the armies included extensive and detailed annexes for air operations, detailing which air units would support which ground units and in what manner. The armies and air services assessed the 1916 campaigns and applied the best practices learned on the battlefield.

In spring 1917, the British and French armies aimed to achieve a grand operational breakthrough at the centre of the German Hindenburg Line at two points: the British Army

French Air Service intelligence officers in 1917, developing the air operations plans for the Nivelle Offensive. Early in the war, all the air services developed their own general staffs and intelligence sections to oversee planning and operations. (Photo 12/Universal Images Group via Getty Images)

**OPPOSITE** THE WESTERN FRONT. SPRING 1917

front at Arras to the north; and to the south, the French front at Chemin des Dames. This breakthrough would enable the envelopment of armies in the central part of the German front, leading to the collapse of the German Army on the Western Front. It was a grand plan supported by maximum effort from the RFC and the French Service Aéronautique, which committed about 40 per cent of their front aircraft to the operation. RFC and French Air Service aircraft significantly outnumbered those of the Luftstreitkräfte. The Allies also had the advantage in numbers of divisions and artillery pieces, and both the British and French armies would use tanks in the offensive.

Facing this onslaught was a German Army that, although outnumbered, held strong defensive positions. They employed their new doctrine of elastic defence, which relied on the placement of reserves supported by mobile artillery groups close behind threatened points at the front and ready for immediate counter-attack. Their defence was also supported by the Air Service, which had been reinforced, and operated under an effective command and communications system that made it flexible.

The grandiose Nivelle plan failed badly. The one bright spot of the offensive was the British success in overrunning the German stronghold at Vimy Ridge on the morning of 9 April, 1917. It was a brilliantly conducted attack where the RFC's support was key to the success. In contrast, the rest of the Nivelle Offensive resulted in heavy losses for both the British and the French armies for little strategic gain, and is remembered infamously as 'Bloody April' because of the loss of more than 200 aircraft shot down in combat, and the death, wounding or capture of more than 300 RFC aircrew. Aside from a few stellar accomplishments by individual flyers, the campaign was a complete failure from an air perspective.

Heavy air losses in April and early May 1917, especially for the RFC but also in the French Air Service, were the result of deficient equipment and training. The spring air campaign serves as a notable example of what happens when one side, albeit outnumbered, enjoys a significant advantage in technology and training.

April 1917 was a high point of the war in terms of German technological advantage. In 1916, the Germans fielded a new series of single-seater fighter planes, initially the Albatros D.I, which quickly evolved into the Albatros D.III. The D.III aircraft were fast, highly manoeuvrable and equipped with two forward-firing machine guns. For this one brief moment of the war, the German fighter force was far superior in quality than its opponents.

The French Nieuport 17 fighter, the main fighter plane for the French in early 1917 and used by some RFC squadrons. Powered by a 110hp Le Rhône rotary engine, it had a maximum speed of 107mph and was fairly manoeuvrable. Armament was one machine gun. It was lethal in the hands of a good pilot, but was outclassed by the Albatros D.III in speed, manoeuvrability and firepower. (IWM Q 67919)

Royal Flying Corps fighter units had squadrons of Nieuport fighters obtained from the French, but were also burdened with slow and obsolete pusher biplanes such as the Airco DH.2 and the two-seater F.E.2s. They were hopelessly outclassed, though a well-flown Nieuport could sometimes get the better of a German Albatros even if the Nieuport had only one machine gun mounted on the aircraft and the Germans had two.

In the SPAD VII, the French had a new fighter faster than the Albatros and with good flying characteristics at lower altitudes, but it was still armed with just a single machine gun.

The Germans also had the technological advantage with their two-seater observation

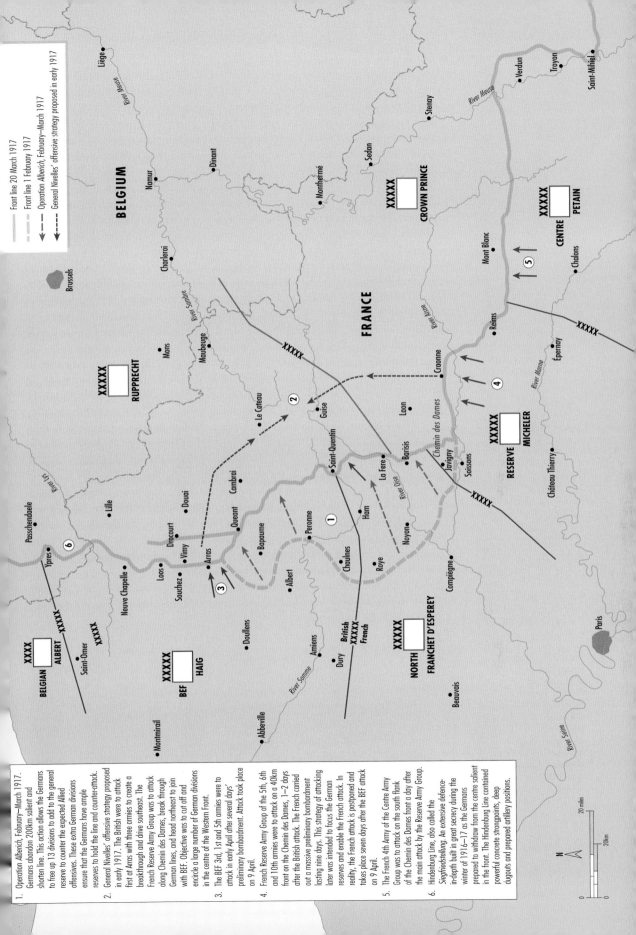

**Legend**

Front line 20 March 1917

Front line 1 February 1917

Operation *Alberich*, February–March 1917

General Nivelles' offensive strategy proposed in early 1917

1. Operation *Alberich*, February–March 1917. Germans abandon 200km salient and shorten line. This action allows the Germans to free up 13 divisions to add to the general reserve to counter the expected Allied offensives. These extra German divisions ensure that the Germans have ample reserves to hold the line and counter-attack.

2. General Nivelles' offensive strategy proposed in early 1917. The British were to attack first at Arras with three armies to create a breakthrough and drive southeast. The French Reserve Army Group was to attack along Chemin des Dames, break through German lines, and head northeast to join with BEF. Objective was to cut off and encircle a large number of German divisions in the centre of the Western Front.

3. The BEF 3rd, 1st and 5th armies were to attack in early April after several days' preliminary bombardment. Attack took place on 9 April.

4. French Reserve Army Group of the 5th, 6th and 10th armies were to attack on a 40km front on the Chemin des Dames, 1–2 days after the British attack. The French carried out a massive preliminary bombardment lasting nine days. This strategy of attacking later was intended to focus the German reserves and enable the French attack. In reality, the French attack is postponed and takes place seven days after the BEF attack on 9 April.

5. The French 4th Army of the Centre Army Group was to attack on the south flank of the Chemin des Dames front a day after the main attack by the Reserve Army Group. Hindenburg Line, also called the *Siegfriedstellung*. An extensive defence-in-depth built in great secrecy during the winter of 1916–17 as the Germans prepared to withdraw from the centre salient in the front. The Hindenburg Line contained powerful concrete strongpoints, deep dugouts and prepared artillery positions.

**BELGIUM**

**FRANCE**

Brussels

Liège

River Meuse

Namur

Dinant

Monthermé

Sedan

Slenay

Verdun

Troyon

Saint-Mihiel

River Meuse

Charleroi

River Sambre

Maubeuge

Mons

Le Cateau

Guise

Laon

Reims

Épernay

Châlons

Mont Blanc

River Aisne

River Marne

River Seine

Paris

Beauvais

Montmirail

Château Thierry

Compiègne

Soissons

Jouvigny

Barisis

Chemin des Dames

Cr: Croonne

Noyon

Roye

Ham

La Fère

Saint-Quentin

Chaulnes

Péronne

Bapaume

Albert

Cambrai

Quéant

Douai

Arras

Vimy

Souchez

Loos

Neuve Chapelle

Lille

Doullens

Amiens

Dury

Abbeville

River Somme

Ypres

Passchendaele

Saint-Omer

River Lys

**XXXXX RUPPRECHT**

**XXXXX CROWN PRINCE**

**XXXXX PETAIN CENTRE**

**XXXXX MICHELER RESERVE**

**XXXXX FRANCHET D'ESPEREY NORTH**

**XXXXX HAIG BEF**

**XXXX ALBERT BELGIAN**

British XXXXX French

20 miles

20km

N

and reconnaissance planes. The sturdy German DFW, LVG and Albatros C.III two-seater reconnaissance planes were highly effective in their reconnaissance and artillery-spotting missions. These aircraft were escorted by armed two-seaters that provided good protection.

French reconnaissance and artillery spotting squadrons were mostly equipped with obsolete Caudron twin-engine bombers, along with Farman-pusher biplanes. Although they lacked the speed and manoeuvrability of the German two-seaters, French reconnaissance aircraft still performed an efficient service.

The RFC still flew a large number of B.E.2 two-seater aircraft, which were quite slow with a top speed of only 75mph, had a low ceiling and were built for stability rather than manoeuvrability. Against the new D.III series of German fighters, the British B.E.2 observation and artillery planes were proverbial sitting ducks, even when strongly escorted. The situation was worsened by the low performance of many British escort fighters. Poor aircrew training also proved especially disastrous for the Royal Flying Corps. The expansion of the RFC had been so rapid that insufficient thought had been given to thorough training of pilots and observers, in major contrast to the French and German air services that required rigorous training of aviators before they were sent into combat. In April 1917, British pilots arrived in France and began flying combat missions with as little as 35 total flying hours. Neither the German nor the French would allow a pilot to go to a front unit without at least twice that number of hours.

After the Allied offensive doctrine failed and the German defensive theory proved to be highly effective, both the British and the French used the experience of the campaign of April 1917 to quickly reform and adapt their tactics and organization. April 1917 saw the RFC introduce two outstanding new aircraft at the front, the S.E.5 fighter (S.E. standing for Scout Experimental) and the Bristol F.2A two-seater fighter/observation plane. Both of these aircraft would re-equip RFC squadrons during the Flanders Campaign, which began in June 1917. That summer would also see the introduction of a new, single-seater fighter, armed with two machine guns like the German fighters, the Sopwith Camel. Changes in equipment, with the replacement of the hopelessly obsolete B.E.2 two-seaters by the much more capable R.E.8s, as well as the improvement in the British fighter force, led to a very different outcome in the air operations of summer 1917. Revamping the training programme at home, which began in 1917, meant that new RFC pilots and observers arrived better prepared for combat. Moreover, new techniques in command and control enabled the British to deal effectively with the German fighter force and observation units.

The Germans, for their part, also changed, adapting and improving their doctrine, evolving the *Schutzstaffel* into ground-attack squadrons that fielded improved two-seater fighters and adapting their fighter organization.

The R.E.8 two-seater observation plane (R.E. standing for 'reconnaissance, experimental') was developed in 1916 and reached the RFC squadrons in early 1917. Powered by a 140hp engine, it had a maximum speed of 98mph and was a huge improvement over the B.E.2 in terms of speed and ceiling. R.E.8s were built in large numbers, but it was difficult to fly and disliked by RFC pilots. (Popperfoto via Getty Images)

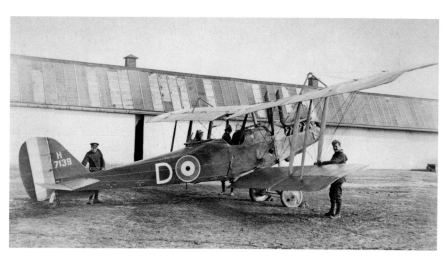

# CHRONOLOGY

## 1916

**October** The German Supreme High Command creates the Luftstreitkräfte to oversee all military aviation. General der Infanterie Ernst Hoeppner is appointed its commander.

**24 October–3 November** The French counter-offensive at Verdun retakes most of the key terrain captured by the Germans in February. The French offensive is led by General Robert Nivelle, commander of the French 2nd Army. Nivelle's aggression and brilliant use of artillery bring him to the attention of the French government.

**November** British and French military commanders end the Anglo–French offensive at the Somme that began in July. One of the main reasons to end the offensive is the loss of Allied air superiority due to the new German Albatros D.I and D.II fighters.

**26 December** General Joseph Joffre, who had served as French Army Chief since August 1914, is relieved from command and General Robert Nivelle is appointed as Army Chief of Staff. Nivelle's appointment is based on his reputation for aggressive action and his advocacy for the offensive.

## 1917

**9 January** German Kaiser Wilhelm formally approves the strategy of the Supreme High Command (*Oberste Heeresleitung*) for 1917.

**January** The German Supreme Command issues directives for a new defensive doctrine for the German Army known as 'elastic defence'.

**January** At a British and French military strategy meeting, General Nivelle proposes an Allied grand offensive in the centre of the Western Front; the British attacking with an army group at Arras, with a French army group to the south attacking on the River Aisne and the Chemin des Dames. The intent is to break through the German defences in two days, envelop the German armies in the centre of the Western Front and annihilate them – thus ending the war in one stroke. General Douglas Haig, commander of the British Expeditionary Force (BEF), is highly sceptical of Nivelle's plan. However, Nivelle's proposals find support among the British and French political leaders.

**9 February–16 March** To support their new defensive strategy, the German Supreme High Command initiates Operation *Alberich*, the planned evacuation of a salient 120km long and 45km wide in the centre of the Western Front. The German armies will withdraw in stages, back to a new defence line, the Hindenburg Line (called the *Siegfriedstellung* by the Germans), a powerful defensive position in depth with numerous concrete fortifications and strongpoints. This evacuation will shorten the German front line by 50km and free up 13 divisions, which can be employed as a strategic reserve.

**15 February** The commander of the French Service Aéronautique, Lieutenant-Colonel Joseph Édouard Barès, is relieved, with Commandant (Major) Paul du Peuty, formerly air commander at Verdun, appointed as the French Air Service commander.

**26–27 February** British and French political and military leaders meet at Calais, where General Nivelle briefs his plan for the grand Allied offensive, to begin in early April. Despite opposition from BEF commander General Haig and senior French commanders, the Nivelle plan is accepted by the British and French governments. In addition, Nivelle is given strategic direction of both the BEF and the French Army for the period of the offensive.

A British observer with his camera mounted on a B.E.2 aircraft *ca.* 1916. During the course of the war, camera equipment developed very quickly in its ability to efficiently photograph large areas of the front. (AC)

**4 March** Allied air reconnaissance spots the German withdrawal for Operation *Alberich*. General Louis d'Espèrey, commander of the French Northern Army Group, requests permission to initiate a French attack in order to disrupt the movement of the German Army. Nivelle denies d'Espèrey's request.

**Mid-March** German air reconnaissance in the Arras sector and behind the French front west of Rheims spot the vast British and French build-up, which signals a major offensive. Forewarned, the German Supreme High Command deploys reinforcements to strengthen those two sectors.

**1–8 April** British and French air reconnaissance activity in the Arras and Chemin des Dames sectors increases in intensity, with a major effort by the French Air Service and RFC to destroy German balloons in the attack sectors.

**4 April** A German trench raid on the French 5th Army front across from the German 7th Army captures a sergeant who is carrying the operational attack plans for three French corps, complete with unit objectives, attack schedules and the artillery support plan. Despite this breach of security, General Nivelle makes no changes to the French attack plans.

**5 April** British artillery preparation for the attack scheduled for 9 April begins on the Arras front.

**6 April** At an Allied strategy conference in Compiègne attended by French President Raymond Poincaré and Prime Minister Ribault, doubts about the upcoming offensive are expressed by General Pétain, commander of Army Group Centre, and General Micheler, commander of the Reserve Army Group. The French prime minister backs Nivelle when the Army Chief of Staff threatens to resign if his offensive plans are called off.

**6 April** The original Nivelle plan called for a British attack to fix the attention of the German Army, with the French offensive to begin one day later. Instead, due to logistics problems, General Nivelle delays the start of the French offensive to 13 April, then to the 16th. The BEF will thus have to fight the German forces alone for a week before the French begin their breakthrough attack.

**6 April** The French Reserve Army Group begins a nine-day artillery preparation along the 41km front on the River Aisnes and Chemin des Dames held by the German 7th and 1st armies. The French barrage is larger than anything yet seen in the war, the French Army employing some 5,300 guns, including 1,650 heavy artillery pieces.

A British heavy howitzer entrenched and camouflaged. Heavy guns like this had the task of destroying strongpoints and countering German artillery. By 1917, camouflage was used by all sides to disguise gun positions. (Niday Picture Library/ Alamy Stock Photo)

**9 April** Three British armies attack the Vimy Ridge and Arras sector, held by the German 6th Army. British divisions attain all of their objectives within hours and push the German front back more than 4 miles with only moderate losses. At Vimy Ridge, the Canadian Corps takes a strong German position, capturing thousands of German prisoners and more than 100 artillery pieces. The 9 April attack is the greatest single-day advance by Allied armies since the beginning of the trench war in 1914. The British advance at Arras creates a crisis for the German Supreme High Command, which is fearful of an Allied breakthrough.

**9–12 April** On the Arras front, the BEF consolidates its position in the newly won territory, but continued attacks make little progress because of the difficulty in bringing up British artillery. German fear of a breakthrough passes as reinforcing divisions are holding the new defence line.

**11 April** In response to the British attack at Arras, the Supreme High Command appoints Colonel Fritz von Lossberg, a noted defensive tactician, as German 6th Army Chief of Staff. Von Lossberg is given complete authority to issue orders to the 6th Army.

**16 April** The French Reserve Army Group begins a massive offensive along 41km of the Chemin des Dames front, with the French 5th and 6th armies putting 200,000 men into the first wave of the attack. After nine days of bombardment, some of the German divisions crack, allowing the French 6th Army to make some advances. In other parts of the front, French corps make no progress. The German 7th and 1st armies employ the new elastic defence doctrine. French 5th and 6th army casualties are heavy, with more than 30,000 on the 16th. The first French tank attack is a complete failure. The German 1st and 7th armies report defences are holding and there is no danger of a French breakthrough.

**17 April** The French 4th Army belonging to General Pétain's Army Group Centre attacks the German 1st Army on the left flank of the Chemin des Dames. As with the French attack the previous day, the 4th Army makes some advances, but casualties are heavy.

**18 April** General von Falkenhausen is relieved of command of the German 6th Army and appointed the military governor of Belgium. General Otto von Below takes over command of the 6th Army.

**16–25 April** Repeated French attacks are met with German counter-attacks by the 7th and 1st armies. There are heavy casualties on both sides. The greatest French advance of the campaign comes on the night of 17 April, when a German corps evacuates the salient before Malmaison, allowing the French a 7km advance and the capture of 100 guns. By 25 April, the French government is alarmed by the lack of progress and heavy casualties in the offensive, and the prime minister seeks to limit further attacks by General Nivelle. Nivelle has deployed the French 10th Army to the front and corps-sized attacks continue.

**29 April** A company of the French 20th Division refuses to go into the battle line, the first instance of a mutiny that will spread through most of the French Army in the next few weeks. The heavy casualties for little gain at Chemin des Dames had effectively broken the morale of the French Army.

**12 April–3 May** The BEF's 1st, 3rd and 5th armies continue to make divisional and army attacks against the German 6th Army. The German 6th Army manages to hold and to counter-attack against the BEF, and casualties on both sides are heavy. In the air, despite being outnumbered, the German qualitative advantage in aircraft allows the Luftstreitkräfte to dominate the skies in the Arras sector. During April, the RFC loses 178 aircraft in the Arras sector.

**4 May** After the failure of an offensive by three British corps on 3 May, the British officially call off the Arras Offensive. Flanders will be the focus of the next British offensive.

**15 May** With the failure of the Nivelle Offensive and mutiny of French units, General Nivelle is relieved as Chief of Staff of the French Army and General Philippe Pétain assumes command, immediately beginning measures to improve the conditions and morale of the French Army, ending the mutiny that affected many divisions. General Pétain also initiates a review of French Army doctrine, vowing to the troops that future attacks will be properly planned and supported.

**2 August** General Pétain relieves Commandant Paul du Peuty as head of the Service Aéronautique and replaces him with Colonel (soon to be General) Charles Duval. Duval will initiate numerous reforms of the French Air Service organization and tactics. Commandant du Peuty requests to return to duty with the ground forces. He is killed in March 1918 leading an infantry battalion.

# ATTACKER'S CAPABILITIES
## The Entente air services in 1917

### The French Service Aéronautique in the Nivelle Offensive

By early spring 1917, the French Air Service had built up to a total of 2,000 aircraft on the Western Front. However, as more than 200 aircraft were assigned to the air defence of Paris, in reality it had approximately 1,800 aircraft to support French armies on the Western Front. Some 1,000 of the available aircraft were organized into reconnaissance and observation *escadrilles* (squadrons), supported by a fighter force of approximately 600 single-seat fighters. A French heavy bomber force of 200 aircraft was also at the front. However, these bombers were concentrated well to the south near Nancy, tasked to conduct long-range bomber raids against the industrial towns of western Germany.

The French Air Service had increased the number of aircraft in each escadrille to ten. The reconnaissance and observation planes were organized into *escadres* (groups) of three escadrilles. French air doctrine assigned one reconnaissance/observation group to each army corps to support its operations. Each reconnaissance/observation escadre had one escadrille to support corps artillery, one to conduct long-range observation photo missions and one to carry out low-level contact flights and provide escort to the artillery and observation planes.

The French fighter force was reorganized, with fighter squadrons organized into groups of three or four squadrons, called a '*Groupe de Combat*'. Most of the French fighter arm was organized into Groupes de Combat (GC). GC 11, 12 and 14 were assigned to support the Reserve Army Group. The three armies of the Reserve Army Group were each assigned one escadrille to fly as close escorts for the reconnaissance/observation groups assigned to each army, allowing the GCs to conduct large patrols deep behind the German lines. In support of the Chemin des Dames Offensive, the French also assigned one bomber wing of 40 aircraft to the French 4th Army Aviation, operating on the flank of the attack. In total, the 15 corps of the Reserve Army Group had 450 aircraft assigned to reconnaissance and artillery observation. The three armies conducting the main attack in April were supported by 150 fighters in the GCs and army fighter squadrons. The 4th Army of General Pétain's Army Group Centre was assigned CG 15, with 30 fighters, and a bomber group (GB 1) of 40 bombers, and had 120 reconnaissance/observation aircraft in its corps support escadrilles. The total French air strength for the offensive on the Chemin des Dames thus numbered about 800 aircraft.

French army aviation also deployed balloon companies of four balloons each to each army. Similarly, the Royal Flying Corps and Luftstreitkräfte deployed balloon companies and detachments at a ratio of one per division in combat. Each French field army aviation commander had an air park for repair and overhaul of damaged aircraft and for receiving replacement aircraft for the front. In spring 1917, the Service Aéronautique had 400–500 aircraft in reserve in the army air parks, ready to replace aircraft lost to operational attrition.

A key part of the French offensive doctrine of 1917 was the employment of the fighter force in the GCs in large fighter formations of two or three squadrons to conduct large patrol sweeps of 20-plus aircraft deep into German territory, up to 50km, in order to tie down the German fighter force and destroy it with their superior numbers.

The French anti-aircraft forces were much smaller than those of the Germans. During the war, the French Army created three large anti-aircraft regiments, but one of these and most of another were assigned to the air defence of Paris, leaving only a few anti-aircraft units available to defend the French balloons and airfields.

## French aircraft

The French fighter force was reformed, and the speedy SPAD VII was finally reaching the front in sufficient numbers to re-equip some of the Nieuport squadrons and to create new fighter squadrons and groups. In February, 268 SPAD VIIs had been received, and more would arrive both before and during the Nivelle Offensive. The French fighter force was the most modern branch of the Service Aéronautique, and in early 1917 most fighter escadrilles were equipped with the Nieuport 17 and 23 biplane fighters (the Nieuport 17 and 23 were virtually the same aircraft, with minor differences). The Nieuport, with a top speed of 110mph, was manoeuvrable, though slightly less so than the Albatros D.III. It was inferior to the German aircraft in other ways, normally carrying only a single machine gun, commonly a Lewis gun mounted on the top wing above the propeller arc. However, after the start of the year, French fighter escadrilles were quickly re-equipped with the sturdy SPAD VII. With a 120mph top speed, the SPAD VII was faster than the Albatros in level flight or a dive, but with the disadvantage of losing its performance above 13,000ft. Like the Nieuport, the SPAD VII was armed with one machine gun, but the SPAD VII had its Vickers machine gun mounted on top of the engine and equipped with a synchronization gear so that it could fire through the propeller. In the hands of a competent pilot, the Nieuports and SPADs could fight the Albatros D.IIIs on fairly equal terms, especially as the French fighter pilot training was thorough and equal to that of the Germans.

A French aircraft radio used by the artillery observer, mounted by the observer's seat. Aircraft could transmit messages in Morse code back to the artillery headquarters, up to 20 miles away. (AC)

The aircraft equipping the French reconnaissance/observation escadrilles were an eclectic mix of airplanes, a considerable cause for concern for the French High Command. Many of the French squadrons were equipped with the two-seater Farman F.40, a slow, single-engine pusher biplane that was thoroughly obsolete by 1917. The greater part of the French reconnaissance

**OPPOSITE** FRENCH AND GERMAN AIRFIELDS. CHEMIN DES DAMES SECTOR, SPRING 1917

squadrons in the Nivelle Offensive flew the twin-engine Caudron G.4, which was originally designed and intended as a bomber. The Caudron G.4 was also obsolescent, underpowered with a top speed of 95mph and lacked manoeuvrability.

In 1916, the French began to build the Sopwith 1½ Strutter under license, and they found the single-engine, two-seater Sopwith to be superior for observation and reconnaissance work to the obsolescent Farmans and Caudrons. The Sopwith 1½ Strutter had a 99mph top speed and was more manoeuvrable, also having an endurance of two hours. The French Service Aéronautique would build and deploy more than 600 Sopwiths as reconnaissance/observation aircraft during 1917, but in April the process of re-equipping squadrons had only just begun. In early 1917, the French had also recently deployed the Caudron G.6 twin-engine aircraft as a development of the Caudron G.4. The G.6 was faster, more manoeuvrable and had better flying qualities than the G.4. A few reconnaissance units were equipped with the newer Letord Let.1 aircraft, a twin-engine bomber modified for artillery observation missions and built in an unusual stagger-wing configuration (unlike most biplanes, the lower wing was placed well forward of the upper wing). The Letords were slightly faster than the Caudron G.4s, but also lacked manoeuvrability. They were so large that they clogged the French airfields, which were now struggling to find space for all the aircraft deployed.

The French bomber escadrilles would play only a small role in the Nivelle Offensive, conducting night raids against German railyards and airfields behind the lines. As in the Somme Offensive, despite the French air commanders' great expectations for bombers in the interdiction role, in reality the night-time raids caused little damage to the Germans.

The SPAD VII, powered by a 150hp Hispano-Suiza engine, was developed in late 1916 and was arriving in significant numbers to the French Air Service in spring 1917. The SPAD VII was the fastest fighter plane in the air in April 1917, exceeding 120mph in level flight, and was also faster than German fighters in a dive. The sturdy SPAD made an excellent gun platform, yet it only carried one machine gun. Its main drawback was that its performance above 13,000ft was mediocre. Nevertheless, the SPAD VII was the most formidable opponent of the Jastas as the Nivelle Campaign opened. (AC)

## The Royal Flying Corps

In spring 1917, the Royal Flying Corps on the Western Front consisted of 57 squadrons, each of 18 aircraft. Eleven squadrons belonged to the Royal Naval Air Service (RNAS), which flew under the operational command of the RFC. The RFC was organized into brigades, each containing air wings made up of three to six squadrons. Each British field army in France was assigned an air brigade to provide all its air support. The air brigades assigned to the Arras Campaign were the 1st Air Brigade, attached to the British 1st Army in the northern

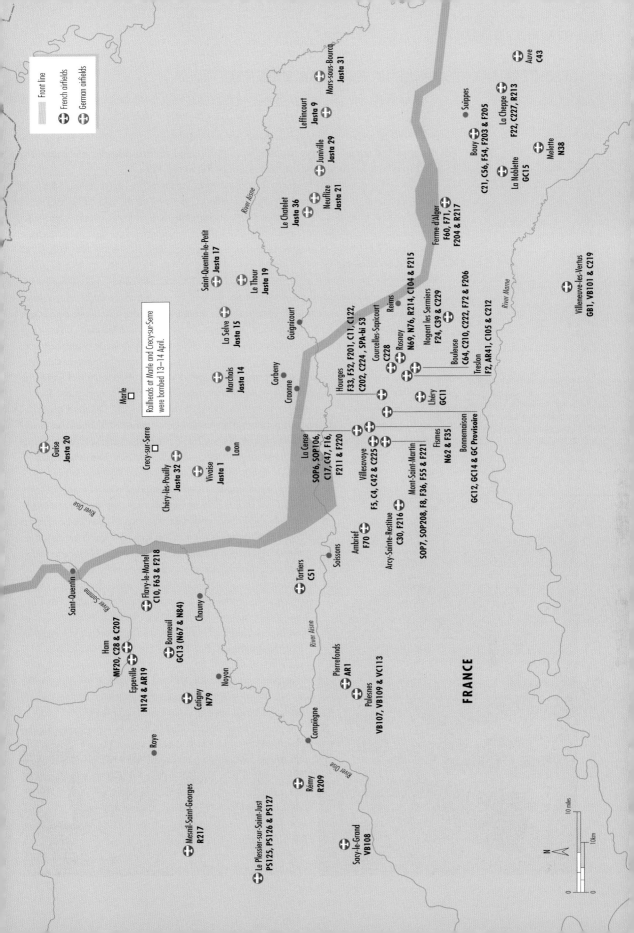

Front line
French airfields
German airfields

Guise
**Jasta 20**

Saint-Quentin

River Somme

River Oise

Flavy-le-Martel
**C10, F63 & F218**

Ham
**MF20, C28 & C207**

Eppeville
**N124 & AR19**

Bonneuil
**GC13 (N67 & N84)**

Chauny

Catigny
**N79**

Noyon

Roye

Mesnil-Saint-Georges
**R217**

Le Plessier-sur-Saint-Just
**PS125, PS126 & PS127**

Rémy
**R209**

River Oise

Compiègne

Pierrefonds
**AR1**

Palesnes
**VB107, VB109 & VC113**

Sacy-le-Grand
**VB108**

River Aisne

Soissons

Tartiers
**C51**

Ambrief
**F70**

Arcy-Sainte-Restitue
**C30, F216**

Mont-Saint-Martin
**SOP7, SOP208, F8, F36, F55 & F221**

Bonnemaison
**GC12, GC14 & GC Provisoire**

Fismes
**N62 & F35**

Villesavoye
**F5, C4, C42 & C225**

La Cense
**SOP6, SOP106,
C17, C47, F16,
F211 & F220**

Vivaise
**Jasta 1**

Laon

Chéry-les-Pouilly
**Jasta 32**

Crecy-sur-Serre

Marle

Railheads at Marle and Crecy-sur-Serre
were bombed 13–14 April.

Marchais
**Jasta 14**

Corbeny

Croonne

Guignicourt

Hourges
**F33, F52, F201, C11, C122,
C202, C224, SPA-bi 53**

Courcelles-Sapicourt
**C228**

Reims

Rosnay
**N9, N76, R214, C104 & F215**

Lhéry
**GC11**

Nogent les Sermiers
**F24, C39 & C229**

Bouleuse
**C64, C210, C222, F72 & F206**

Treslon
**F2, AR41, C105 & C212**

La Selve
**Jasta 15**

Saint-Quentin-le-Petit
**Jasta 17**

Le Thour
**Jasta 19**

Le Châtelet
**Jasta 36**

Neuflize
**Jasta 21**

Juniville
**Jasta 29**

Leffincourt
**Jasta 9**

Mars-sous-Bourcq
**Jasta 31**

River Aisne

Ferme d'Alger
**F60, F71,
F204 & R217**

River Marne

Villeneuve-les-Vertus
**GB1, VB101 & C219**

Suippes

Bouy
**C21, C56, F54, F203 & F205**

La Cheppe
**F22, C227, R213**

La Noblette
**GC15**

Melette
**N38**

Auve
**C43**

**FRANCE**

N

10 miles

10km

## OPPOSITE BRITISH AND GERMAN AIRFIELDS. ARRAS SECTOR, SPRING 1917

part of the sector; the 3rd Air Brigade, assigned to the 3rd Army, which had the longest part of the front and would bear the brunt of the fighting; and the 5th Brigade, attached to the 5th Army, which fought on the southern flank of the Arras sector.

The 1st, 3rd and 5th air brigades had been strongly reinforced in February and March to meet the demands of the campaign. Approximately 40 per cent of the RFC units in France were committed to the Nivelle Offensive. Not only were the flying wings of the RFC brigades reinforced with extra squadrons, but additional balloon companies were sent to the balloon wings of each RFC brigade as well, to ensure that each division in combat would have an observation balloon.

The RFC in France consisted of five air brigades, with the headquarters of the RFC having a wing with six squadrons and two large aircraft depots, as well as a command that managed engine repair shops, all backed up by the air supply command. At the start of the campaign, the RFC brigade air parks had a reserve of 300-plus aircraft to replace losses.

The main aircraft of the RFC in the corps support role was the hopelessly obsolete B.E.2, which equipped 15 squadrons. Ten squadrons flew the F.E.2 two-seater fighters, which were also obsolete and would be used in the campaign as night bombers. Two squadrons from the fighter force flew Airco DH.2 pusher fighters, which stood little chance in combat against the German Albatros.

The Royal Flying Corps had only a few observation squadrons with adequate two-seat observation planes. Three squadrons now had the new R.E.8 two-seaters, equal in performance to the German DFW and LVG aircraft, and one squadron was equipped with the new Armstrong Whitworth F.K.8 two-seater. Four squadrons were equipped with the Sopwith 1½ Strutter, which was fairly capable, although in contrast to the French, the British tended to use it as a two-seat fighter rather than an observation plane. One squadron had been equipped with SPAD XIIs and XXs, French two-seater observation planes that were quickly phased out due to poor flying qualities.

The first squadron equipped with the Bristol F.2A two-seat fighter would see action in the Spring Campaign. The RFC fighter force in France included six squadrons of the highly manoeuvrable Sopwith Pups, which belonged to RNAS squadrons. The RNAS 10th Squadron, which flew with the RFC's 3rd Brigade, was equipped with the highly manoeuvrable Sopwith Triplane, an aircraft so admired by the Germans that they copied it. Along with the S.E.5, the Germans considered it a dangerous opponent.

In April, four British squadrons were equipped with the Nieuport 17; one F.E.8 squadron was transitioning to the Nieuport and another to the SPAD VII. Britain's newest fighter, the S.E.5, equipped the new No. 56 Squadron and would see its first action on the Arras front in April. With the exception of No. 56 Squadron, all British single-seat fighters had just one machine gun, putting them at a considerable disadvantage to the Germans.

At the start of the year, Major General Hugh Trenchard, commander of the RFC in France, was rightfully concerned

A French balloon being raised. In the German, British and French Armies, a stationary balloon was allocated to each division in the line. (AC)

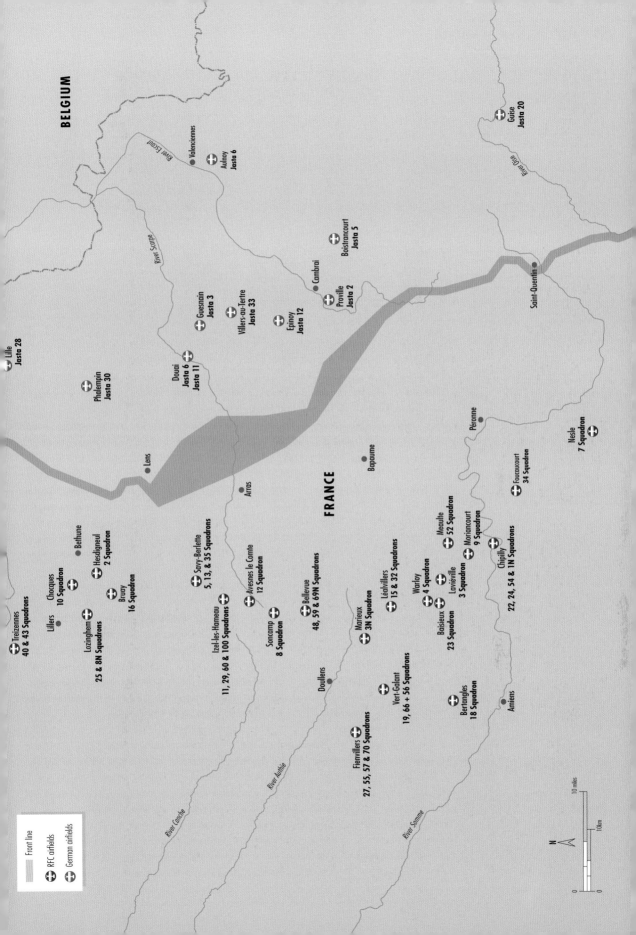

BELGIUM

FRANCE

River Escaut

River Scarpe

River Oise

River Canche

River Authie

River Somme

Lille
Jasta 28

Phalempin
Jasta 30

Douai
Jasta 6
Jasta 11

Lens

Arras

Bapaume

Valenciennes

Aulnoy
Jasta 6

Boistrancourt
Jasta 5

Cambrai

Proville
Jasta 2

Guesnain
Jasta 3

Villers-au-Tertre
Jasta 33

Epinoy
Jasta 12

Saint-Quentin

Guise
Jasta 20

Péronne

Nesle
7 Squadron

Foucaucourt
34 Squadron

Chipilly
22, 24, 54 & 1N Squadrons

Moriancourt
9 Squadron

Meaulte
52 Squadron

Lavieville
3 Squadron

Warloy
4 Squadron

Baisieux
23 Squadron

Bertangles
18 Squadron

Amiens

Doullens

Vert-Galant
19, 66 + 56 Squadrons

Fienvillers
27, 55, 57 & 70 Squadrons

Marieux
3N Squadron

Lealvillers
15 & 32 Squadrons

Bellevue
48, 59 & 69N Squadrons

Soncamp
8 Squadron

Izel-les-Hameau
11, 29, 60 & 100 Squadrons

Avesnes le Comte
12 Squadron

Savy-Berlette
5, 13, & 35 Squadrons

Bethune

Hesdigneul
2 Squadron

Bruay
16 Squadron

Chocques
10 Squadron

Lillers

Lozinghem
25 & 8N Squadrons

Treizennes
40 & 43 Squadrons

Front line

RFC airfields

German airfields

N

10 miles

10km

The Sopwith Triplane first flew in 1916 and equipped four RNAS squadrons in 1917. Powered by a 130hp rotary engine, it had a maximum speed of 117mph and a very fast climb rate. It was more manoeuvrable than an Albatros and was armed with one machine gun. German pilots were so impressed with the plane when they encountered it on the Arras front, that the Germans copied the design. The RNAS soon took it out of service as it was difficult to maintain and the upper wing could fail. (Museum of Flight/ Corbis via Getty Images)

about not only the obsolescence of the aircraft that constituted the majority of RFC stock in France, but also the state of pilot and observer training. In January, Trenchard had appealed to General David Henderson, commander of British military aviation in London, for a major revision to the RFC pilot and observer training. RFC pilots had been arriving at front units with about half the flying hours of a French or German pilot. Moreover, while the French and Germans had extensive specialized courses for their air observers, most RFC observers flying for artillery support were volunteers from the Royal Artillery, who had some training in the RFC observation squadrons but nothing approximating a professional course. At Trenchard's insistence, not only was the RFC pilot training programme revised, but in early 1917, specialist courses for observers were created. These important reforms would be of great value to the RFC later in the year. However, in the spring of 1917, the RFC was short of properly trained pilots and observers.

The three RFC brigades supporting the Arras attack in April were all organized into two air wings, each consisting of four to six squadrons, and one balloon wing with three to four companies. In each brigade, one wing was equipped with squadrons flying two-seat observation aircraft, mainly the B.E.2. However, the R.E.8 was also present in the RFC's 3rd Brigade. The second wing of the three air brigades in the campaign consisted of single-seat and two-seat fighter squadrons, including a mix of the obsolete F.E.2 fighter squadrons, Nieuport 17s and Sopwith 1½ Strutters. The RFC's 5th Brigade, supporting the 5th Army, had two F.E.2 two-seater squadrons, with No. 23 Squadron transitioning to the SPAD VII, along with one squadron of DH.2s and one RNAS Squadron equipped with Sopwith Pups. A total of some 450 aircraft were assigned to support the three armies, with the RFC's 3rd Brigade supporting the British 3rd Army – with ten squadrons and 180 aircraft – as the largest brigade on the Arras front, which was appropriate as the 3rd Army would bear the main burden for the offensive.

Trenchard's air plan drew on the Somme experience, as well as that of the French at Verdun. Trenchard would order a bombing campaign against the German airfields, headquarters and railheads. Influenced by French air commander Commandant de Peuty, Trenchard copied the French practice of flying large patrols deep in the German rear. Two-thirds of the fighter force would patrol over the first 15km forward of the front line, where most of the observation and artillery flights would take place and where the B.E.2s required escorts. The other third of the British fighter squadrons would be deployed on patrols deep into German territory, up to 50km behind the German lines, thus forcing the Germans into combat. Unfortunately for the RFC, it was a strategy that worked to the advantage of the Germans, who were employing their new Schutzstaffeln to protect and escort their reconnaissance and artillery flyers operating on the front lines. Consequently, eight German Jastas operating in the 6th Army area were free to counter any British incursions behind the front.

# Senior commanders

## General Robert Nivelle

General Robert Georges Nivelle (born 1856) was the author of the grand offensive plan that bears his name. In 1914, Nivelle, a professional artillery officer, was serving as a colonel and commander of an artillery regiment. His excellent performance in the first battles of the war earned him promotion to brigadier general in October 1914. Nivelle, moreover, spoke perfect English thanks to his English mother. He also had a distinguished record before 1914, having served in combat in North Africa.

Moving up quickly as a division and corps commander in 1915, Nivelle was promoted to command of the 2nd Army on the Verdun front. He perfected his artillery techniques during the Verdun Campaign, most notably the creeping barrage. Nivelle was famed as the most aggressive general in General Pétain's army group. The victorious attack of his 2nd Army at Verdun in October 1916, which drove the Germans out of key terrain they had seized at the beginning of the battle, was one of the few bright points for the Allied armies in 1916 and brought him considerable national attention. When Marshal Joseph Joffre resigned as French Army Chief of Staff in December 1916, Nivelle was jumped ahead of army group commanders like Pétain to head up the French Army. Nivelle then began pushing his plan for the two-pronged British and French attacks which he claimed would quickly bring decisive victory and end the war.

General Robert Nivelle, Chief of Staff of the French Army from December 1916–May 1917. (Bettmann/Getty Images)

Nivelle's concept of operations revolved around his expertise with artillery. He believed that with his artillery techniques and massive preparatory bombardment, along with the support of tanks, the German front could be broken in a mere two days. From the start, BEF Commander General Haig and the other senior French Army generals were doubtful of the plan, arguing that the entire concept was wildly over-optimistic. Yet, despite the open doubts of both Haig and General Micheler, the army group commander whom Nivelle had appointed to lead the attack on the Chemin des Dames, Nivelle convinced both British Prime Minister Lloyd George and his French counterpart Alexandre Ribot at the February Allied strategy conference that his plan was workable.

At a final conference on 6 April 1917 that included General Pétain, Prime Minister Ribot and President Raymond Poincaré, Nivelle refuted the doubts about the offensive by insisting that he would resign if his plan was not given final approval. The political leaders thereupon endorsed Nivelle.

As predicted by his critics, the Nivelle Offensive was a grand failure – especially for the French Army. It broke the morale of the French Army, leading to company-sized mutinies in late April 1917 and larger-scale mutinies throughout the French Army in May and June that year. The final result was Nivelle's relief from command on 17 May 1917, being replaced as Army Chief of Staff by General Pétain.

A group of French Schneider tanks at the Chemin des Dames before the first tank attack by the French Army on 16 April. (IWM Q56454)

While a brilliant artilleryman, Nivelle was certainly no strategist. He was described by Bernard Serrigny, who had served on Pétain's staff, as a 'limited soldier': 'War was for him a scientific matter. He claimed to treat it like an equation, to define the final formula for victory, a technician above all, never having had any high-level role, neither on the General Staff nor in the forces. He must have been quickly overwhelmed in his position of authority.' Serrigny observed the overwhelming tactical mentality of Nivelle, noting that he was using only 1:5,000-scale maps to direct operations and did not have maps of the entire front. In his formulaic approach to planning, Nivelle failed to note that his German enemies also got a vote in the overall strategy and might have plans and tactics of their own to nullify the tactics that Nivelle had used successfully at Verdun. Nevertheless, Nivelle exuded total confidence in his plan. His failure to call off the offensive in the early stages, when it was already clear that no breakthrough was possible, was the final straw for the long-suffering French infantrymen, provoking them to mutiny.

### Colonel Joseph Édouard Barès

Born in 1872, Joseph Édouard Barès served as director of the French Army Service Aéronautique from September 1914 to February 1917. Although no longer commanding the French Air Service during the Spring 1917 Offensive, Barès should be regarded as one of the central figures of military aviation in World War I and the primary architect for the success of the French Air Service in 1918.

Colonel Joseph Édouard Barès, commander of French military aviation August 1914–February 1917. (AC)

Joseph Barès was commissioned as a naval infantry officer in 1894 and saw combat in the colonial campaign in Madagascar. He was a graduate of the Army Staff College, and in 1909 was one of the first officers to join the French Air Service. From 1909 to the outbreak of the Great War, Barès was intimately involved in all aspects of French military aviation. When General Joffre appointed him as head of the Service Aéronautique, Barès was promoted to colonel and immediately started laying down plans for the large-scale expansion of the French Air Service. At the very beginning of the war, Barès laid out the missions of the air service as being reconnaissance, artillery spotting, bombing and fighting other aircraft. In autumn 1914, he met with the chief engineer of the Hispano-Suiza Engine Company and endorsed the production of the revolutionary 150hp in-line aircraft engine that would provide the Allied military aviation with a significant technological advantage over the Germans.

As with other air service commanders, Barès faced a constant battle with the War Ministry as to the types and models of aircraft to be produced for the French Army. At the urging of the War Ministry, in 1915 and 1916,

A Royal Aircraft Factory F.E.2 biplane. This was a pusher biplane like the DH.2, armed with one machine gun and served as a fighter, observation plane and light bomber. It was adequate in 1916 but obsolete in 1917. The RFC used it largely as a night bomber during the spring 1917 battles. (Photo by Hulton Archive/ Getty Images)

contracts had been made to build a large number of bombers to strike behind German lines in a strategic air campaign. As a result, Barès had a large number of obsolescent aircraft. Though slow and ungainly, carrying poor bombloads, in the 1917 campaign they proved useful in the reconnaissance and aerial spotting role, which had now become the main focus of military aviation.

Fighting War Ministry production policies that resulted in too many models of mediocre aircraft, Barès promoted a policy of ruthless standardization in late 1916 and early 1917 to concentrate upon building only a few high-performance aircraft models suitable for mass production, which would provide the Service Aéronautique with the numbers of aircraft necessary to overwhelm the Germans. On Barès' initiative, aircraft such as the SPAD XIII fighter, Bréguet 14 bomber and Salmson 2A2 reconnaissance plane were all under development by early 1917. By the end of that year, those superb aircraft, produced in large numbers, would equip not only the French Air Service, but its new American allies, providing the coalition with the right aviation forces for victory in 1918.

In addition to overseeing the development of the flying units, Barès ensured that from the start of the war, France had a comprehensive training system for observers and pilots. When Barès was forced out as Chief of the Service Aéronautique in February 1917, he took over the role of coordinator of all air units for General Pétain's army group and was therefore involved in the southern flank of the Chemin des Dames battle. After the war, Barès would serve two terms as Chief of Staff of the French Air Force in the early 1930s.

## Major General Hugh Trenchard

The commander of the RFC in France from 1915–18, Hugh Trenchard was commissioned as an infantry lieutenant in the 1890s and served in the Indian Army. As a young officer, Trenchard was known far more for his athletic prowess than for any intellectual accomplishments. During the Boer War, Trenchard served as an infantry officer in South Africa and distinguished himself as a capable combat leader. He was gravely wounded by a bullet to the chest, which required a long period of recovery.

After the Boer War, Trenchard served in Nigeria and again won notice for leading his troops in suppressing colonial rebellions. Despite his impressive record as a combat soldier, Trenchard's career was stagnating when, in 1912, he joined the fledgling Royal Flying Corps and learned to fly. In contrast to his indifference to study as a young army officer, Trenchard applied himself enthusiastically to learn about aviation. Upon the outbreak of the Great War, Trenchard, now a major, commanded the RFC Home Garrison while the RFC combat squadrons deployed to France. However, Trenchard was soon in the middle of combat when, now promoted to colonel, he took command of the 1st Wing of the RFC serving with the BEF.

During the 1915 campaign in Flanders, Trenchard met General Douglas Haig, then a corps commander, and began a process of educating Haig about what the RFC could do to provide reconnaissance and support to ground troops. The Trenchard–Haig relationship lasted throughout the rest of the war, with Trenchard serving as a loyal subordinate to Haig, and Haig relying upon Trenchard and the RFC partners. When Haig replaced General John French as BEF commander in 1915, Trenchard was promoted and made Chief of the RFC in France. Haig understood that the war between 1915 and 1918 was fundamentally one of attrition, and that victory would not be possible until the German Army was simply worn down to breaking point. This form of warfare required an unrelenting offensive by the British Army to gain and hold the initiative on the battlefield.

For Trenchard, Haig's relentless ground offensive had its counterpart in an unyielding air offensive. Both Haig and Trenchard have been heavily criticized for this policy, which also resulted in heavy losses for the attacker. On the other hand, it is hard to argue with success, for it was the attritional war strategy that eventually worked and wore down the German Army to provide the eventual Allied victory in 1918.

Though inarticulate both in speech and writing, Trenchard established a close rapport with the officers and men of the RFC, and especially good relationships with his Allied counterpart air commanders, first with the French and then with the Americans. Trenchard travelled constantly to meet with his pilots, observers and ground crews, working ceaselessly to find out what the problems were from the perspective of the men flying at the front. Trenchard – who was always accompanied on his trips to air units by his aide, British journalist and author Maurice Baring – took note of the concerns of his pilots and commanders. Turning to his aide, he would direct, 'Take that down, Baring.' Baring would quickly turn Trenchard's notes and conversations into well-written memos and directives.

Major General Hugh Trenchard, commander of the RFC in France 1915–18. (Universal History Archive via Getty Images)

German bombs rigged to the underwing bomb rack of a light bomber. German and Allied aircraft were modified to carry bombs early in the war. Shown here are light, 20kg bombs. (AC)

Going into the Spring 1917 Campaign, Trenchard was very well aware of the problems and deficiencies of the RFC. In talks with his corps support squadrons, Trenchard learned of the haphazard training of observers and pilots. In early 1917, his pressure resulted in the revamping of the RFC's pilot–observer–aircrew training programmes, as well as the subsequent improvement in the capability and qualifications of RFC pilots and personnel before the end of the year.

As an Allied leader, Trenchard demonstrated a great deal of sensitivity and understanding. Throughout the war, he collaborated very closely with his counterparts in the French Air Service. Indeed, he adopted the lessons the French were learning at Verdun and applied them to the RFC. Trenchard also formed a close personal friendship with Commandant Paul du Peuty, the French Army's Air Commander in 1917, and their two air services strove to support one another throughout the war. Trenchard and General Haig made sure that the French Air Service was supplied with the excellent Lewis gun and the Vickers heavy machine gun, which equipped aircraft such as the SPAD VII and SPAD XIII and were much more suitable as aircraft armament than the French machine guns. The French, for their part, ensured that extra Nieuport 17s and SPAD VIIs were made available to equip British squadrons, at a time when the British fighter planes were hopelessly outclassed by the Albatros D.IIIs.

In 1918, Trenchard served briefly as chief of the new Royal Air Force before resigning that position and taking command of the Allied independent bomber force, conducting a strategic bombing campaign against the Germans. After World War I, Hugh Trenchard would serve for a decade as RAF Chief of Staff. He is regarded to this day as a key figure in shaping British military aviation.

## Commandant Paul du Peuty

Born in 1878, Commandant Paul du Peuty served as commander of the Service Aéronautique from February 1917 to August 1917. Commissioned as a cavalry officer in 1890, du Peuty saw extensive combat in Morocco during the 1911–13 pacification campaign. When the war broke out in 1914, du Peuty volunteered for military pilot training and upon obtaining his wings assumed command of the newly formed MS 48 Squadron.

Commandant Paul du Peuty. (AC)

Du Peuty was a capable and aggressive pilot and leader. He was decorated in 1915 for an aerial combat in which he and his observer were both wounded yet still managed to attack German aircraft, despite more than 100 bullet holes in their own plane. With the creation of the French fighter force in 1915, du Peuty became a fighter commander. He served on the Somme in 1916 and came into close contact with the RFC, becoming friends with RFC commander General Trenchard. Du Peuty was promoted to commandant (major) and assumed command of the French 10th Army aviation units at Verdun, where he worked with General Nivelle. Du Peuty had an enthusiasm for the offensive that mirrored Nivelle's own aggression. Instead of engaging the Germans close to the front lines, du Peuty believed that massed fighters should operate 50km or more behind the German lines in order to control the entire air space over the German Army.

On 15 February 1917, Nivelle made du Peuty commander of the Service Aéronautique at the front. In the coming offensive, du Peuty saw his mission as ensuring complete air superiority over the Germans. He worked closely with the RFC to share ideas, equipment and plans. Unfortunately, du Peuty's concept of massing fighters in large groups and sending them deep behind the German lines proved to be a complete failure. Despite their superior numbers, French fighter forces failed to engage the Germans on the front lines. Left with little fighter protection, the French corps aircraft suffered serious losses from German fighters.

Once Nivelle was removed in May 1917, du Peuty would not last much longer as Air Commander for the French Army. In August 1917, the new Chief of Staff, General Pétain, replaced du Peuty with Colonel Charles Duval, who would reorganize and retrain the Service Aéronautique and lead it to eventual victory in 1918. Although offered the position of Chief of Fighters by Duval, du Peuty chose to return to the ground forces. He was killed in action on 30 March 1918 leading a battalion of Zouaves in a counter-attack against the German spring offensive. Paul du Peuty was respected as a brave and competent officer by French airmen and his RFC counterparts. However, du Peuty was limited in his understanding of airpower, having been associated only with the fighter force during his career as an air leader, never showing any real aptitude or understanding for the other missions of aviation.

## Army air commanders

The German and Allied air forces produced some outstanding officers who served as army-level air commanders in the Spring 1917 Campaign. Luftstreitkräfte and Royal Flying Corps army air commanders showed remarkably similar backgrounds. Of the German army flying commanders (*Kommandeur der Flieger*, or *KoFl.*) and the British RFC brigade commanders (each army was assigned one RFC brigade to support its air efforts), all were middle-aged officers born between 1875 and 1885, giving them an average age of 40. Both British and German commanders had solid records in the pre-war armies and air services.

The operational air commanders were an exceptional group of officers, the creation of military air services having attracted officers with a highly technical bent. Moreover, the German and British senior air commanders all began the war as *Flieger Abteilung* or squadron commanders. They had thus seen extensive aerial combat and had all been decorated for their aerial exploits in 1914–15. All had worked their way up through the chain of command to reach the higher levels of air service leadership.

## British RFC brigade commanders

The commander of the RFC 3rd Brigade, Brigadier General Jack Higgins (born 1875), led the force that saw the brunt of combat in 1917 in what became known as 'Bloody April'. Higgins, an artillery officer before joining the RFC in 1912, had been involved with the RFC's first experiments in mounting machine guns on aircraft. Higgins flew as a squadron commander at the start of the war and was wounded, then being promoted to wing commander. He took command of the RFC's 2nd Brigade in 1915, and the following year was appointed brigadier general commanding 3rd Brigade. Higgins had observed successful French operations in the counter-attack at Verdun in October and, like Trenchard, was strongly influenced by the successful French tactics of that campaign. Higgins ended the war with a permanent rank of RAF air marshal and had a long and distinguished career in aviation.

The commander of the RFC 1st Brigade (supporting the British 1st Army), General Gordon Shephard (born 1885), was the youngest of the senior air commanders in the April battles. He joined the RFC in 1912 and worked his way up through squadron and wing command before being posted to command of the 1st Brigade in February 1917. Shephard would go on to command RFC units in the Flanders Campaign but died in January 1918 when he crashed a Nieuport fighter. The RFC's 5th Brigade commander was Charles Longcroft (born 1883). Like his counterparts, he too had joined the RFC in 1912 and moved up through squadron and wing command.

# DEFENDER'S CAPABILITIES

## The Luftstreitkräfte: German Imperial Air Service

Upon the formation of the Luftstreitkräfte in October 1916, German military aviation underwent a thorough reorganization in preparation for the 1917 battles. The new plan for the German Air Service was to provide a large air force for the Western Front. In April 1917, the Luftstreitkräfte on the Western Front contained 81 *Artillerie Flieger Abteilungen* (AFA, artillery aviation flights) of six aircraft each, with 27 Flieger Abteilungen specializing in observation and photo reconnaissance, also of six aircraft each. There were 37 Jastas (short for *Jagdstaffel*, fighter squadrons) of 12 aircraft each, and 30 Schustas (*Schutzstaffel*, protection squadrons), each a flight of six aircraft, as well as three heavy bomber wings and three bomber squadrons. There were also 17 air parks, one assigned to each army at the front. Altogether, they held 300-plus aircraft in reserve as replacements for expected combat and operational attrition. The air parks also received aircraft shipped from factories for distribution to front units.

The German Air Service's total strength on the Western Front in spring 1917 amounted to about 1,600 aircraft. Most of the force, 852 planes, were single-engine, two-seater reconnaissance and observation aircraft. The 30 Schutzstaffel were about 10 per cent of the total force, and 444 single-seat fighters constituted another 30 per cent. The Luftstreitkräfte was in the process of building a heavy-bomber force, consisting of 100 twin-engine and even some four-engine heavy bombers. The bomber force's main aircraft was the Gotha G.IV twin-engine bomber, capable of carrying a 500kg bombload. The German bomber force also fielded the AEG G.IV twin-engine bomber. German heavy bombers would play no role in the spring campaign because the large bomber wings were in Flanders being readied for the upcoming strategic bombing campaign against Britain.

The Schutzstaffel were small squadrons with the primary duty of providing escorts for the artillery and reconnaissance aircraft, thereby freeing the Jastas to concentrate on their mission of contesting Allied reconnaissance and fighters.

The Gotha G.IV heavy bomber. Fielded in 1917, its two 260hp engines gave it an unimpressive top speed of 83mph, but it had long range and carried 500kg of bombs. This was the main aircraft of the German heavy bomber units and played a prominent role in the 1917–18 interdiction campaigns as a night bomber. (AC)

The Luftstreitkräfte also had command of the German anti-aircraft units. By 1917, the Germans had deployed more than 1,200 light and heavy flak guns, usually organized into platoons of three or four guns. During the course of the war, the Luftstreitkräfte came to place a higher priority on the development of ground-based air defence – flak forces – than the Allied Powers. The German flak units early in the war were equipped with modified 77mm field guns, but by 1917 the flak arm of the Luftstreitkräfte fielded specially designed anti-aircraft guns with better shells and fuses. Some of the 77mm heavy flak guns were mounted on trucks to make them highly mobile weapons. Probably the deadliest German flak gun was a modified 37mm automatic cannon that had originally been designed for the protection of German naval vessels. The 37mm cannon was only effective against low-flying targets up to 4,000ft. As artillery spotters and observation planes operated at low altitude, the 37mm was an exceptionally dangerous adversary.

## Luftstreitkräfte organization in the 1917 campaign

A German 77mm motorized flak gun. The German Army developed a much larger specialist anti-aircraft force than either the French or the British. The Germans also employed more advanced anti-aircraft guns. The 77mm motorized flak gun was a purpose-built, high-velocity, rapid-fire gun. (AC)

Each German army was assigned an air commander (*Kommandeur der Flieger*, or *KoFl.*), who commanded all aviation and flak assets for that field army. One addition to the Luftstreitkräfte organization was the deployment of *Luftschutz* (air defence) officers. With their small teams of two NCOs and four enlisted men, the Luftschutz officers would set up a ground observation post 4–5km behind the front line, usually co-located with a flak platoon. Equipped with a theodolite and high-powered telescopes, each Luftschutz officer's team was to monitor and report on the number, type, altitude and direction of all Allied aircraft crossing the lines. The Luftstreitkräfte created the post of group commander, a major innovation in command and control. Each group commander was normally aligned

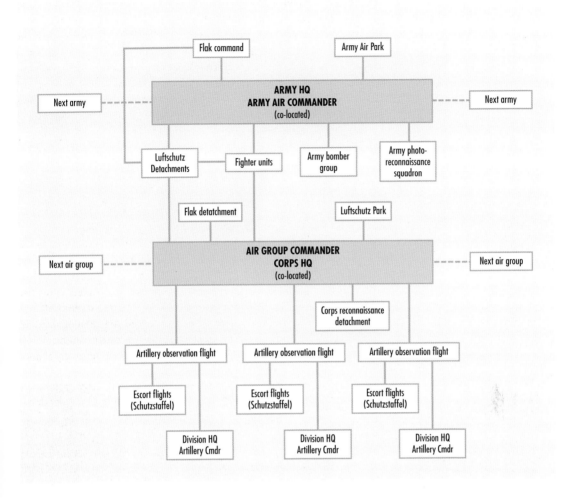

**ABOVE** LUFTSTREITKRÄFTE COMMUNICATIONS AND CONTROL NETWORK, SPRING 1917

During the winter of 1916-17, the Luftstreitkräfte developed a highly effective command-and-control network for the air units assigned to support the field armies. The Imperial Air Service possessed its own signal units to ensure that the group air commanders and their staffs assigned to support the army corps, and the flak and fighter units under command of the Army Air Commander, were connected by telephone and radio. Group commanders and the Army Air Commander were co-located with the corps and army headquarters they were supporting to ensure information was shared.

A major innovation was the Air Defence Officer (*Luftschutzoffizier*) with a team of NCOs and signallers stationed near the front line. Connected by telephone and radios to air groups, fighter and flak units and the army headquarters, these forward teams noted all Allied air activity over the front and reported on numbers, types, direction and altitude of Allied squadrons crossing the lines. This information enabled the Jastas to engage Allied airmen on favourable terms.

The Army Air Commander passed reports from the Army Weather Service on wind direction and speed at various altitudes to the Jastas which, in turn, would use this information to ambush the Allied patrols using tailwinds to gain extra speed in their attacks.

The extensive communications network ensured the German air and ground commanders had an accurate awareness of the air situation throughout the battle and German units were given timely warnings of Allied air missions into their territory.

A German Forward Signals Centre close to the front. The Germans placed a Luftschutzoffizier (Air Defence officer) with a team of two NCOs and four privates in observation posts close to the front. Air Defence officers, equipped with telescopes, monitored and reported air activity over the front. The Air Defence officers were usually located with flak units and were tied into the army and air communications net. Thanks to the Air Defence officers and the Luftstreitkräfte's signals network, German air commanders had a good awareness of all air activity in their sectors. (AC)

and co-located, along with his own staff and communications, with a corps headquarters at the front. The group commander's mission was to oversee all air operations in the corps sector.

During the winter of 1916–17, the Luftstreitkräfte created an extensive telephone and radio signals network to facilitate the coordination of all air units and close cooperation with army, corps and division headquarters. The Luftschutz officers, flak units, Schutzstaffel and Jastas were tied into the communications net, with group commanders co-located with their associated corps headquarters and the army air commander co-located at the army headquarters. The Luftstreitkräfte's signals network enabled fighter squadrons to be notified immediately of Allied air patrols so that a quick response could be mounted. The signals network also allowed for information on Allied air activity to flow immediately to all the flak units in that army's area of operations.

In spring 1917, the German 6th Army in the Arras sector and the German 7th and 1st armies in the Chemin des Dames sector placed their artillery flyer sections and Schustas under the control of the group commander, who also controlled all the flak platoons and air observation posts in the corps sector. Each group was normally assigned three or four artillery flights, allowing for one flight to support each division in combat. Each air group commander also had an observation/photo reconnaissance flight to support corps operations. One to three Schustas were assigned to each air group in the German armies, to be used at the discretion of the air group commander, usually employed for escort duties but sometimes, as the campaign developed, in the ground-attack role against enemy troops. The air commanders of the German 7th and 1st armies assigned their fighter squadrons to the air groups, each air group controlling one or two Jastas. The German 6th Army air commander, with five air groups, followed the same group plan as the 7th and 1st army air commanders for observation and artillery flights and Schustas. However, the Jastas assigned to the 6th Army were not placed under the group commanders to operate in corps sectors, but were assigned missions directly by the army air commander. This explains why fighter operations in the German 1st and 7th army areas were concentrated close to the front, contesting the French observation aircraft and their escorts, while in the 6th Army area, German fighter units such as Jasta 11 contested British patrols far behind the lines.

## German aircraft

In autumn 1917, the German Supreme High Command, under Generals Hindenburg and Ludendorff, assigned new aircraft and engine production goals to support a major expansion of the Luftstreitkräfte. The Hindenburg Plan of 1916 set a production demand of 1,000 aircraft per month for the German Army and Navy. However, due to the inefficiencies of the German aircraft manufacturers, with too many models being produced in small contracts, it was only in spring 1917 that the Germans began to meet their goals. Consequently, German air units on all fronts were chronically short of aircraft. The number of serviceable German aircraft on the Western Front was closer to 1,300 than the official strength of 1,600 in April 1917. The consistent problem with aircraft production meant that in most German squadrons there was a mix of aircraft models.

In the German fighter force, the excellent Albatros D.III, superior to any Allied fighter aircraft, predominated, rounded out by the Albatros D.II and Roland D.II and D.III fighters, aircraft with similar characteristics. The Schustas were equipped with single-engine, two-seater aircraft such as the Albatros C.III and the AEG I. The Albatros C.III, at this time the most common aircraft in the Schustas, was soon followed by an improved model, the Albatros C.V.

The German artillery and photo reconnaissance units were equipped with a variety of two-seater, single-engine biplanes, predominantly the LVG C.II and the DFW C.II, as well as the Albatros C.III. The German LVG and DFW C.IIs were sturdy and reliable aircraft with a top speed of 105mph. They were fairly manoeuvrable, with good performance at both low and high altitudes. The aircraft equipping German observation and artillery units were generally superior to their British and French counterparts. The German star performer in the photo reconnaissance role was the Rumpler C.IV, a high-altitude reconnaissance aircraft. With its modified, high-compression 240hp Maybach

The Albatros C.III was used by German observation units and equipped many of the Schustas in spring 1917. The Albatros C.III was fast and manoeuvrable. Its performance in the Schustas encouraged the Luftstreitkräfte to expand the use and the role of those squadrons. (IWM Q 105758)

A Roland D.III fighter. German fighter squadrons had several different fighter models on hand in 1917 and 1918. The Roland D.III was a single-engine fighter plane with a plywood fuselage, with similar characteristics to the Albatros D.III, and was found in several German Jastas in 1917. It was a very capable fighter plane, but only a few hundred were ever built. (IWM, Q 66462)

engine, the Rumpler C.IV could reach an altitude of 20,000ft. Both pilot and observer had electrically heated flight suits to combat the extreme cold at high altitude, also carrying bottled oxygen to deal with the thin air. The Rumpler C.IV could fly long distances far above the ceiling of any Allied fighter, and was far out of the range of any anti-aircraft guns. Upon reaching the target area, the observer could flick a switch that allowed the special automatic camera to take a photograph every ten seconds. Thus, on a clear day, German photo reconnaissance could map a strip of several kilometres. Due to its high-altitude performance, the Rumpler CL.IV was rarely shot down by Allied fighters. The Luftstreitkräfte assigned one CL.IV to each photo reconnaissance Flieger Abteilung to conduct long-range missions in support of a field army, or even the Supreme High Command. Later, the Luftstreitkräfte High Command would organize the Rumpler reconnaissance planes – replaced by the Rumpler CL.VII later that year – into specialized long-range reconnaissance units.

In spring 1917, although heavily outnumbered by the French Air Service and the RFC, the Germans generally had better aircraft, manned by well-trained pilots and observers. The Luftstreitkräfte had also addressed the training of flak officers and crews, as well as the Luftschutz officers and NCOs. In 1915, Colonel Hermann von der Lieth-Thomsen had already set up a special school for officers, and NCOs were assigned to the flak units. Air defence officers and NCOs also underwent a special training course.

In the runup to the Spring Offensive, the Luftstreitkräfte had strongly reinforced the German 6th, 7th and 1st armies, which were all obvious targets for the Allies. The major air battles had already begun in late March. At the beginning of the British offensive at Arras, the German 6th Army aviation commander had at his disposal 224 reconnaissance/air protection and fighter aircraft, 170 of which were reported operational on 7 April. The 6th Army aviation had been reinforced from 14 balloon detachments to 19, with one balloon normally assigned to support each division in contact. In early April, the German 6th Army had six observation detachments, 14 artillery detachments, six Schustas and six Jastas. On 11 April, the German Supreme High Command, concerned regarding a possible breakthrough on the Arras front, reinforced the German 6th Army with one photo reconnaissance detachment, two artillery detachments, three Schustas and two Jastas, bringing the total aircraft on the 6th Army front to 282. Before the French attack on 16 April, the 7th and 1st army aviation groups had also been strongly reinforced, as those areas were quiet sectors until the French build-up in March 1917. The German 7th Army aviation under Walter Starr contained four air groups that controlled 18 reconnaissance and artillery air detachments, eight Schustas and six Jastas, totalling 202 aircraft. The German 1st Army, which would face an attack by the French 4th Army of General Pétain's Army Group Centre, was organized into four air groups and contained 15 reconnaissance and artillery detachments, ten Schustas and five Jastas, for a total of 192 aircraft. Thus, the 392 aircraft of the two German armies on the Chemin des Dames front would face off against approximately 800 French aircraft. German air forces on the Arras front had an official strength of 282 planes facing more than 400 British aircraft in the three RFC brigades supporting the campaign.

# Senior commanders

### Generalleutnant Ernst von Hoeppner

When Generals Hindenburg and Ludendorff took over the Supreme High Command of the German Armed Forces in August 1916, one of their first tasks was reorganizing the German Air Service. At that time, command of the Air Service was divided between the Chief of Field Aviation, in charge of the flying units at the front, and the Inspectorate of Military Aviation in Berlin, in charge of aircraft development, production and research. The Supreme High Command believed all German aviation forces and organizations should be under a single unified leadership, and in October 1916 established the *Luftstreitkräfte* (Imperial Air Service), an air force with a single commander and its own general staff to command all aspects of military aviation, subordinate only to the Supreme High Command.

The Luftstreitkräfte included all the ancillary aspects of military aviation, including balloons, anti-aircraft guns, airships and signals units. Hindenburg and Ludendorff selected General Ernst von Hoeppner (1860–1922) to command the Luftstreitkräfte. Von Hoeppner was a cavalryman with a distinguished record of service on the General Staff, and had already been a division commander and chief of staff of a field army. He was not an aviator, but he was trusted by the Supreme High Command for proven competence as a senior commander and problem-solver. Von Hoeppner justified this faith immediately, initiating a programme of reorganization and expansion of the Luftstreitkräfte. Army aviation commanders were reorganized with group commanders and new group headquarters, all tied into an extensive command-and-control network.

Von Hoeppner took the view of a strategic-level commander and wisely left actual daily command and direction of the Air Service to his able Chief of Staff, Colonel Hermann von der Lieth-Thomsen, who by 1917 had already been associated with German military aviation for nine years. Von Hoeppner was a good learner and listener, travelling constantly to the air units on the front and ready to speak with group and squadron commanders, and pilots and observers, getting their recommendations for equipment and tactics. In early 1917, von Hoeppner oversaw an

Luftstreitkräfte Commander General der Infanterie Ernst von Hoeppner visiting a German heavy bomber unit in Flanders in the summer of 1917. (AC)

Colonel Hermann von der Lieth-Thomsen, Luftstreitkräfte Chief of Staff. (AC)

effective force reorganization, but also the publication of new doctrine for both offensive and defensive aerial operations.

Von Hoepper took especial interest in the creation of a new strategic bomber force composed of the heavy Gotha G.IV bombers and even larger, four-engine Riesen bombers, which carried out the bombing campaign against Britain from May 1917 until early 1918. Von Hoeppner served as Luftstreitkräfte commander to the end of the war, retiring shortly after.

### Colonel Hermann von der Lieth-Thomsen

Born in 1867, Colonel Hermann von der Lieth-Thomsen was commissioned in 1887 as a Pioneer (engineer officer) and was selected for the elite General Staff Academy. He later served on the General Staff in Berlin, where he earned a reputation for exceptional competence in technical issues. He entered the world of military aviation in 1908 when, as a major, he was appointed to head a new special technical section of the General Staff which would advise on military aviation. From this point, Lieth-Thomsen became intimately involved in all German military aviation development. In 1914, he was serving as Inspector of Airships.

When the war began, the German Air Service consisted of field aviation detachments operating under the direction of each corps, with no real unified leadership other than the Aviation Inspectorate on the General Staff in Berlin. Thus, in March 1915, the German High Command created the position of *Chef des Flugwesens* (Chief of Aviation), which would command all aviation units flying in support of the German Army. Lieth-Thomsen, who already personally knew most officers involved in German military aviation, took this position, with promotion to lieutenant colonel. From 1915 into 1916, Lieth-Thomsen oversaw the massive growth of the German Air Service and the expansion of field aviation units into specialized squadrons. Like his counterpart French and British Air Commanders, he too engaged in constant battles with the War Ministry over the types of aircraft required at the front and the technical developments that needed to be implemented by the ministry.

Most importantly, Lieth-Thomsen was a stickler for thorough aviation training; at his direction, a whole series of training schools were created, not only for pilots, observers and artillery pilots, but also for anti-aircraft specialist officers and signals officers. Due to Lieth-Thomsen's emphasis on training, the Luftstreitkräfte would maintain a significant advantage over the British and French for most of the war. Lieth-Thomsen remained in his position as chief of staff of the Luftstreitkräfte when it was formed in 1916. As Chief of Staff, he selected the the senior army and group air commanders and squadron commanders who led the successful German air effort throughout 1917. Von der Lieth-Thomsen retired after the war, but his status as one of the pioneers of German military aviation was recognized. Even though by the 1930s he was legally blind, he was promoted to the rank of general in the Luftwaffe and given special honours by the new German air force to emphasize its link with the old Luftstreitkräfte.

# German Army aviation commanders

Hauptmann (Captain) Walter Starr (born 1882) was commander of the German 7th Army Aviation that bore the brunt of the French offensive on the Chemin des Dames. Starr, commissioned in 1901 as an artillery officer, joined the Air Service in 1913 and trained as an observer, then as a pilot. He began the war as a pilot, becoming a Flieger Abteilung commander in early 1915. He served as an air group commander in 1916 and took command of 7th Army Aviation in February 1917. In 1918, Starr served in senior staff positions on the Luftstreitkräfte General Staff. He remained in the army after the war and served in its secret Luftwaffe in the 1920s. In the 1930s, he was promoted to general in the Luftwaffe.

Commanding the aviation force of the German 1st Army on the southern flank of the Chemin des Dames Offensive was Hauptmann Wilhelm Haehnelt (born 1875). Haehnelt was an infantry officer who had gone through the elite German Army General Staff course and become a member of the General Staff Corps. His first experience in aviation was training in 1908 as a balloon observer. In 1911, he became one of the first cadre of pilots in the German Imperial Air Service. At the beginning of the war, Haehnelt commanded the air detachment of the German 1st Army during the invasion of France and was decorated for his performance in the 1914 battles. In 1916, Haehnelt held senior staff position in the Luftstreitkräfte Headquarters, and he was appointed 1st Army Air Commander in early 1917. Like Starr, Haehnelt had a distinguished post-war career as an aviator, becoming a Luftwaffe general in the 1930s.

A German 37mm automatic anti-aircraft cannon. This rapid-fire cannon was probably the most dangerous weapon employed by German flak units. (AC)

The German 6th Army Aviation Commander, Captain Maximilian Sorg, had served as a Flieger Abteilung commander from the start of the war. In 1915, he was decorated for his combat exploits that year. As Air Commander for the 6th Army, Sorg bore the brunt of the RFC's offensive at Arras.

It should be noted that, while commanding an equivalent number of aircraft and air units, and with roughly the same experience, RFC brigade commanders held the rank of brigadier general while their German counterparts had the rank of captain. In the German military system, where promotion came very slowly, this was not unusual. Nor was this a disadvantage, for in the German Army command authority came from position held and not from official rank. Thus, during the Arras battle in April, Colonel Fritz von Lossberg could take over as Chief of Staff of the 6th Army and issue direct orders to lieutenant general corps commanders without any doubt that his orders would be immediately obeyed, despite the difference in formal rank.

RFC Commander Hugh Trenchard and Luftstreitkräfte Chief of Staff Hermann von der Lieth-Thomsen showed good judgment in picking their senior air commanders, relying on the small cadre of officers who had been with the military aviation in the pre-war force. The army aviation commanders had the technical understanding and experience in flying that ensured that both sides would quickly adapt equipment and tactics to the rapidly changing nature of the air war.

# AIRPOWER IN 1917

## The eyes of the big guns

Four Airco DH.2 single-seat fighters in France in 1916. Some of the hopelessly obsolete DH.2 pusher biplanes were still flying with the RFC in the spring 1917 battles. It was an adequate aircraft for the first stages of the Somme Campaign, but the arrival of the Albatros D.I fighters immediately made it obsolete. While the pusher biplanes were efficient, having the engine behind the pilot restricted the pilot's rear field of vision. Unfortunately for British pilots, striking from the rear was the favoured means of German attack. (Mirrorpix via Getty Images)

More than anything else, World War I was centred on the use of artillery, which inflicted more than 80 per cent of all the war's casualties. From late 1914, artillery dominated the battlefield as heavily fortified trench lines, including deep dugouts and concrete strongpoints, became the new norm of warfare. Only by a massive application of artillery firepower did infantry have a chance to break through successive trench lines. The artillery force in each army rapidly grew in size. The French Army put great effort into fielding new medium and heavy artillery pieces, including the excellent 155mm cannons, which had a significantly longer range (16km), fired heavier shells and were more effective in destroying enemy fortifications. The new family of heavy artillery included the British 60-pdr gun, effective not only in destroying fortifications with heavy shells, but also having enough range to counter the enemy's artillery. Along with the traditional targets of enemy troops and fortifications, the medium and heavy artillery also had the task of countering the enemy's artillery and installations behind the lines, including headquarters, supply points and assembly areas. If the attackers' artillery could suppress enemy artillery and reduce the strongpoints, their infantry could break through without excessive losses. Infantry units were reorganized to include many light machine guns, light mortars and rifle grenades that could help them break into enemy lines and outflank strongpoints if well supported by artillery. Conversely, if enough of the defender's artillery managed to survive the attacker's preliminary bombardment, an infantry attack would be stopped cold with massive casualties.

### Aircraft and the artillery

At the outset of the war, aircraft had the primary mission of reconnaissance for the ground forces. With the introduction of vast trench lines, stretching along the Western Front from the Swiss border to the North Sea, aerial reconnaissance became more important than ever.

To be effective, artillery required accurate maps and up-to-date, detailed target information. Aerial photography became a highly developed art in the German and Allied armies, with thousands of aerial photographs processed every week. Each photo was first analysed to spot enemy fortifications, installations and supply points, and the information was used to develop detailed, small-scale maps. Ground commanders used these maps to plan attack and defence, and the artillery used them to develop accurate map-grid coordinates for their firing data.

As aerial observation by both sides became pervasive, armies adapted, learning to camouflage their rear-area installations. As attested by many period photographs, gun batteries were now camouflaged, with their artillery pieces firing from positions covered in camouflage netting. Armies also built dummy gun positions, with wooden mock-up guns and poor camouflage, to divert the attention of enemy airmen and artillery.

A French 400mm railway gun from 1917. France, Britain and Germany took massive guns made for coastal defence and mounted them on rail cars. Firing shells over 500kg, they were exceptionally destructive to enemy strongpoints. (Alamy)

## Fixed balloons and the artillery

A major means of aerial artillery observation for all World War I armies was the aerial balloon, filled with hydrogen and attached to the ground by a heavy cable. When weather permitted, the balloon observer – an experienced artillery officer – could ascend to as high as 4,000ft, from where, with a telescope, he could observe enemy activity, especially noting troop movements or gun flashes from artillery. Balloon observers, connected to artillery headquarters, provided targets and directed fire. Balloon units were part of the aviation forces and set up their balloons 15km behind their own front lines, where they could observe activity up to 6km behind the enemy's first trench line.

A British wooden dummy gun in a fake gun position. Aerial reconnaissance was so ubiquitous that Allied armies set up false gun emplacements to be seen by enemy air reconnaissance, which would then attract German artillery fire, allowing the counter-battery force to then target their opponents. (Alamy Stock Photo)

As prominent targets for enemy aircraft, balloons were surrounded by light anti-aircraft guns and heavy machine guns, which made them an especially dangerous target for fighter planes to attack. Because of this, until 1918, balloon observers were the only airmen of World War I to have a parachute as standard equipment. If aircraft attacked his balloon, the observer could leap to safety. 'Balloon busting', as it was called, became something of an art for some fighter pilots. In clear weather, any fighter attacking a balloon could be easily spotted, tracked and targeted by a host of anti-aircraft guns. Accordingly, pilots learned that the best time to attack the balloons was at dawn or dusk, when the poor light and haze gave cover and, hopefully, they could evade detection until the moment of the attack. 'Balloon-busting' was considered so important that any pilot shooting down a balloon received the same credit as for bringing down an airplane.

The standard organization of the Allied and German air services included one balloon company per corps, with one balloon per division. Destruction of enemy balloons was a priority mission for the German and Allied fighter units during the Arras and Chemin des Dames battles.

Although effective, balloon observation had its drawbacks. Observers in balloons, unlike aircraft, were limited in observing behind hills and ridgelines, and were much less effective in the essential mission of spotting enemy artillery positions than airplanes.

A French balloon observation officer observing German activity with binoculars. Balloon observers were artillery officers in balloons approximately 15km behind the lines. Balloons could ascend to 3,500–4,000ft. From there, using telescopes and binoculars, a balloon observer could observe up to 4 miles behind enemy lines. Balloon observers were connected directly to artillery headquarters by telephone. Most artillery missions were directed by balloon observers. (AC)

## The artillery flyers

In 1917, the top priority for the aviation forces was to support the artillery. Using aircraft to direct artillery fire was very much in the minds of the pre-war aviation services. Early experiments were conducted to place radios in aircraft, but the weight of radios before 1914 made this impractical. Yet, like aviation technology, radio technology evolved very quickly from the outbreak of the war. Radios available in 1914 were heavy affairs, requiring large generators or batteries beyond the carrying capacity of aircraft of the day. It was likewise impractical to put radio receivers in aircraft because they were excessive in size and weight. The large radio receivers, along with the generators required to operate them, were normally carried in a motorized vehicle or large horse-drawn wagon. Military units would commonly erect a collapsible antenna, usually about 10m tall. In order to receive transmission, these antennas might have to be extended to a height of 80ft. Radio-receiving stations took considerable time to set up, erecting the mast being a complicated affair.

The solution was to develop radio transmitters small and light enough to mount in airplanes, which would be capable of sending Morse-code messages to a receiving station located at artillery headquarters. By 1915, experiments with small radio transmitters powered by small generators proved that observers could direct artillery fire from the air with great accuracy.

However, as there was no way to mount a heavy receiver in an aircraft, the observer had no means to receive radio messages. Still, one-way radio traffic worked well enough. An observation aircraft equipped with a transmitter connected to a 50-metre antenna wire that trailed below the aircraft could transmit in Morse code to the artillery headquarters for 20 miles or more.

The aviation forces developed practical and simple methods to transmit information from observers to the artillery. An aerial observer would normally be assigned to a corps and tasked to observe targets in a specific zone. Flying with a 1:10,000 or 1:20,000 map divided into lettered squares, the observer would identify targets and transmit Morse messages to the artillery. The procedure used by all combatants was a Morse message system in which the observer would identify the grid square and the type of target using a simple two or three-letter Morse combination. Upon receiving this target reference, the artillery would fire a registration round at the reference provided. Using a standard code with two or three letters signifying distance, direction, target type and so on, a good observer could quickly adjust fire and bring accurate mass fire onto a target.

By late 1916, the greater part of the two-seater reconnaissance planes that constituted most air services' aircraft were committed to the artillery mission. It was important that observers be well-trained, so Germany and France had special observer courses. Observers had to learn precise navigation and map-reading and develop the ability to determine targets even in poor visibility. The French required artillery observers to be trained artillery officers. An observer had to operate at low-to-medium altitude equipped with binoculars, in order to accurately identify likely targets. In addition to navigating and directing artillery fire, the observer had the secondary task of manning the machine gun mounted to the observer's cockpit to protect his aircraft from enemy fighters. The two-seater observation craft were often pressed into service as a light bomber, carrying 50–100kg of bombs.

Artillery flyers typically flew the two-seater reconnaissance aircraft, although the French would employ twin-engine and three-seat bombers in the role. By 1917, the British, French and Germans had all developed larger, more powerful high-performance aircraft for the artillery observation role, but many obsolete aircraft could still be found in observation squadrons.

*Installation de C.S.F.*

A French Army radio truck *ca.* 1917. While a radio transmitter powered by a small generator was light enough to put in an airplane, a radio receiver was a large affair, requiring generators, batteries, a large receiving set and a telescoping antenna at least 30ft tall. By 1916, radio signals detachments were found in the artillery headquarters of every army. (AC)

A German Morse code key for artillery flyers. An artillery pilot could transmit messages to the artillery headquarters using two- or three-letter codes to identify the target location and type of target. This basic system was used by all British, French, and German artillery flyers during the war. (AC)

## Auszug aus dem Schlüsselheft.(1)

### Zeichen für Artilleriefliegerdienst

| Für F.T. | Meldung | Sichtzeichen |
|---|---|---|
| s | Schuß | |
| s? | Ist geschossen worden? | |
| ss | Salve (Batterie geht zum Salvenfeuer über) | |
| ps | Pollgolve | |
| ef | Einzelfeuer (Batterie geht wieder zum Einzelfeuer über) | |
| ns | Es wurde nicht geschossen | |
| ff | Batterie feuerbereit | |
| nh | Nach Hause (Flieger ist entlassen oder ich fliege zum Flughafen zurück) | |
| ou | Beobachtung unmöglich | |
| wa | Wer ist feuerbereit? (Welche Batterie steht zur Verfügung?) | |
| nz | Neues Ziel (Vorschlag zum Zielwechsel oder Batterie nimmt vorgeschl. Zielwechsel vor) | |
| wi | Batterie geht zum Wirkungsschießen über | |
| fe | fremde Einschläge am Ziel | |
| zz | Sichtzeichen erbeten | |
| az | Aufschlagzünder | |
| bz | Brennzünder | |
| z | Ziel | |
| zm | Zielmitte | |
| zr | Ziel rechts | |
| zl | Ziel links | |
| w | Weit | |
| k | Kurz | |
| wk | Im Ziel (±)beim Einzelschuß | |
| sw | Sehr weit | |
| sk | Sehr kurz | |
| wn | Weit, nahe am Ziel | |
| kn | Kurz nahe am Ziel | |
| r | Rechts | |
| l | Links | |
| tr | Treffer | |
| al | Allgemeine Schußlage | |
| no | Nicht beobachtet (nicht gesehen) | |
| fr | fraglich | |
| va | Warten (Batterie vorübergehend nicht feuerbereit) | |
| nv | Nicht verstanden | |
| vo | Verstanden | |
| ja | Ja | |
| ne | Nein | |

### Morsezeichen und Buchstabieralphabet

| | | |
|---|---|---|
| a | Adolf | ·— |
| b | Berta | —··· |
| c | Cäsar | —·—· |
| d | David | —·· |
| e | Emil | · |
| é | Französ. e | ··—·· |
| f | Friedrich | ··—· |
| g | Gustav | ——· |
| h | Heinrich | ···· |
| i | Isidor | ·· |
| j | Jakob | ·——— |
| k | Karl | —·— |
| l | Ludwig | ·—·· |
| m | Moritz | —— |
| n | Nathan | —· |
| o | Otto | ——— |
| p | Paula | ·——· |
| q | Quelle | ——·— |
| r | Richard | ·—· |
| s | Siegfried | ··· |
| t | Theodor | — |
| u | Ursula | ··— |
| v | Viktor | ···— |
| w | Willi | ·—— |
| x | Xantippe | —··— |
| y | Ypsilon | —·—— |
| z | Zacharias | ——·· |
| ä | Adolfemil | ·—·— |
| ö | Ottoemil | ———· |
| ü | Ursulaemil | ··—— |
| ch | Cäsarheinrich | ———— |

### Ziffern:

| | |
|---|---|
| 1 | ·———— |
| 2 | ··——— |
| 3 | ···—— |
| 4 | ····— |
| 5 | ····· |
| 6 | —···· |
| 7 | ——··· |
| 8 | ———·· |
| 9 | ————· |
| 0 | ————— |

### gekürzt:

| | |
|---|---|
| 1 | ·— |
| 2 | ··— |
| 3 | ···— |
| 5 | ··· |

### Satz und Hilfszeichen:

| | |
|---|---|
| Punkt | ··—·—·— |
| Komma | ——··—— |
| Fragezeichen | ··——·· |
| Binde -oder Gedankenstrich | —····— |
| Klammer | —·——·— |
| Bruchstrich | —··—· |
| Trennungszeichen | —···— |
| Irrungszeichen | ········ |
| Wartezeichen | ·—··· |

Although fighter aces were the heroes of the media, the worth of expert artillery flyers was recognized by their respective high commands. Several of the most successful German artillery flyers received Germany's highest decoration, the *Pour le Mérite* or Blue Max, for providing effective artillery spotting for the army. The French also decorated their expert artillery flyers, awarding different grades of the *Légion d'Honneur* (Legion of Honour) to their pilots.

The work of the artillery flyers required them to cross enemy lines, and they often flew their vital support missions in very marginal weather. The ideal altitude for artillery spotting was considered to be 4,000–6,000ft, close enough to make out target details but sufficiently high to evade machine-gun fire from the ground. Since artillery spotting was essential to the army, they were also a special target for enemy fighters, so artillery flyers were often escorted by a flight of single-seat or two-seat fighters to protect them.

## Lessons from the Verdun and Somme Campaigns

In winter 1915–16, the German Air Service was in a strong position on the Western Front. The Fokker E.III Eindecker, with its forward-firing machine gun with a synchronization gear enabling it to fire through the propeller, was able to dominate the skies over the front. In 1915, specialized fighter forces started to appear on both sides. As 1916 began, the Germans planned to use their airpower to support a major ground offensive.

General von Falkenhayn, the German Army Chief of Staff, planned a major offensive in the quiet Verdun sector in eastern France with the intent of destroying the French Army by attrition. In February 1916, a German army group launched a massive attack to overrun the old French border fortifications and draw the French Army into a desperate defensive battle. The intent of the Verdun Campaign was not the traditional manoeuvre and encirclement strategy to destroy the enemy army, but rather to draw the French into a giant artillery trap, where the German superiority in heavy guns could massively damage the French Army.

To support this offensive, the Germans massed 164 aircraft, mostly two-seater observation planes, supported by Fokker fighters and some bombers. At first, the German offensive was quite successful, seizing key terrain and fortifications. However, General Pétain, the French army group commander for the Verdun sector, insisted that the line be held and stiffened the French resistance.

A French airfield near Verdun 1916–17. Note the complexes of hangars, repair shops, barracks and fuel storage. (Alamy)

Caudron R.4, an improved version of the Caudron G.4 bomber, served in several French reconnaissance escadrilles in spring 1917. (FLHC 2021A/Alamy Stock Photo)

The Germans held air superiority for the first weeks of the campaign with greater numbers, which allowed German reconnaissance and artillery to operate mostly unmolested. The Germans set up a system of standing patrols to dominate the air over the front and keep the French from interfering with German observation. General Pétain then called on French airman Major Charles de Tricornot de Rose to form a French fighter force to break German air superiority. At this time, the French were starting to field a brand-new fighter plane, the Nieuport 11, a biplane in a sesquiplane (one wing half (or less) the area of the other) arrangement, powered by a 110hp rotary engine and equipped with a machine gun, normally a British Lewis gun, mounted atop the wing so that it was able to fire over the arc of the propeller. The Nieuport 11 was considerably faster than the Fokker Eindecker, with a 15mph speed advantage. The Nieuport was also more manoeuvrable than the Eindecker and, with one machine gun, matched the Germans in firepower.

Major de Tricornot de Rose developed an aerial strategy to counter the Germans. The French broke the air blockade by massing between ten and 15 new Nieuport fighters to sweep through the front, engaging the German patrols. The Nieuport proved far superior to the previously feared Fokker Eindecker. These large French fighter patrols allowed their reconnaissance and artillery pilots through to do their mission. French air superiority thus made the French artillery much more effective, and also allowed bombers to bring the German rear areas under attack.

The French and Germans also employed multi-engine bombers to attack each other's key industries in 1915 and 1916. The Germans used their AEG bombers in raids against French munitions factories in Nancy and French rail centres around Verdun. In like manner, the French bomber force – with Farman, Voisin and Caudron aircraft – struck at industrial targets in western Germany. However, for both the Allies and the Germans, the bomber campaigns failed to produce actual results as the early-war bombers employed were slow, underpowered and capable of carrying only small bomb loads. Still, for all the air services the idea of bombing the enemy rear was an attractive one, and the bomber forces would grow and improve in 1917 with larger aircraft and engines capable of carrying loads up to 500kg.

## Lessons from the Somme, July–November, 1916

Britain and France's offensive on the Somme began on 1 July 1916. The British conducted the main attack, the French launching a secondary offensive on the southern sector of the Somme. Both the French and Germans concentrated their air services at the Somme, and

A Sopwith 1½ Strutter two-seater observation plane. The Sopwith 1½ Strutter appeared in 1916 and was the first British aircraft to fly with a forward-mounted, synchronized machine gun. The RFC used the Sopwith as a two-seat fighter as well as in observation and light bombing roles. The French Air Service used it in the corps reconnaissance role. Although obsolescent in 1917, the French continued the process of re-equipping their corps observation squadrons with the Sopwith throughout 1917. The Sopwith featured here is in French service. (Jacques Boyer/Roger Viollet via Getty Images)

at the beginning of the campaign the German Air Service was simply overwhelmed. The RFC – which had learned the lessons of an aggressive offence from the French – maintained a constant offensive posture that, for more than two months, ensured air superiority and allowed the British reconnaissance and artillery aircraft to do their work.

What enabled Allied air superiority was the French Nieuport fighters and the appearance of new fighting aircraft in the ranks of the RFC. In winter 1915–16, the British fielded a new purpose-built fighter, the Airco DH.2, which was a pusher biplane, meaning that the propeller faced the rear. The machine gun mounted in front therefore did not require a synchronization gear, which was important as the early models of German, French and British synchronization apparatuses tended to malfunction, introducing the danger that a pilot could shoot off his own propeller. The DH.2, along with the two-seater F.E.2, also a pusher biplane, had a speed equal to the Fokker Eindecker and was highly manoeuvrable. The British also fielded a new two-seater multi-purpose aircraft, the Sopwith 1½ Strutter, an aircraft also adopted by the French Air Service. The Sopwith 1½ Strutter had a forward-firing machine gun with synchronization gear, the first British aircraft to be fitted with such apparatus. In the rear, the observer was also armed with a machine gun. With a top speed of 97mph, it had a 10mph speed advantage over the Fokker.

In the first two months on the Somme, the RFC conducted its mission effectively. Yet the offensive was still a failure as the BEF had overestimated the result of its long bombardment of German lines and had failed to effectively target the German artillery at the opening of the battle. After the initial attack, the British army commanders continued to push forward. From July to November, the Somme became a series of large battles, with high casualties for both sides and only incremental ground gains for the Allies.

The RFC at the Somme also carried out an extensive bombing campaign of German rear areas, with railheads being the primary target. Lacking heavy purpose-built bombers at the time, the RFC used two-seater observation craft, such as the B.E.2, in bombing missions. With a 200lb load of small bombs (the observer had to be left behind due to weight limits), the RFC carried out night attacks. Pilots flying the night missions reported fires and explosions, with heavy damage to the German rear. In fact, little damage occurred from small raids of ten aircraft carrying small bombs. After the war the Germans compared their loss and damage records with Allied bomber reports. Only 5 per cent of British bomber raids had inflicted any serious damage to the Germans.

Airpower played a key role in ending the British offensive on the Somme in November 1916. From June until mid-September, Allied air superiority had been so pronounced that the German Army commanders complained that their troops were suffering from low morale: every time they looked up, they saw Allied aircraft overhead and rarely, if ever, any German aircraft countering them. This changed in September 1916 when the Germans fielded a new fighter organization, the *Jasta* or *Jagdstaffel* (Hunting Squadron), equipped with the latest new aircraft, the Albatros D.I. The Albatros D.I had a sleek, streamlined appearance and its plywood fuselage was very sturdy. Its 160hp Mercedes or Benz engine could push the aircraft to 105mph, which gave it a speed advantage over every Allied fighter plane. Moreover, this fast and manoeuvrable aircraft carried two machine guns, firing forward and synchronized through the propeller. In the hands of a competent pilot, Allied fighters and the slow observation craft were fairly easy prey.

The introduction of the Albatros D.I was soon followed by improved D.II and D.III models. The new German Jagdstaffel organization combined and reorganized the fighter flights, which had consisted of six aircraft. Late 1916 saw dramatic changes in French, German and British squadron organization. While German observation and artillery-spotting flights and bombers were organized into a flight (*Abteilung*) of six aircraft, the new fighter Jastas had 12 aircraft and 14 pilots. The French had adapted their fighter flights into escadrilles of ten aircraft each. Three or four of these squadrons would be grouped as an escadre under a single commander. The British began the year with squadrons of 18 aircraft, each squadron being a multi-purpose organization. Any squadron might contain three or four aircraft models, such as the Morane-Saulnier, used as fighters or escorts, and include B.E.2s or Martinsyde two-seaters for observation, reconnaissance and spotting. A squadron could be given a spotting or photographic mission and would provide its own escort. After the Battle of the Somme commenced, the logistics of maintaining several different types of aircraft in one squadron became too difficult. By autumn 1916, the RFC was reorganized, with each squadron having only one type of aircraft to ease maintenance issues. Fighters became specialized in air-to-air battles, while two-seater squadrons conducted spotting, photo reconnaissance or bombing missions.

The B.E.2 two-seater observation plane. The B.E.2 was developed from a pre-war design and served from 1915 to mid-1917 as the primary observation aircraft of the RFC. Approximately 3,500 of these sturdy biplanes were built. The B.E.2 was used for photo reconnaissance, artillery flying and also as a light bomber. The B.E.2 was underpowered, had a low ceiling and a maximum speed of 75mph. It was hopelessly obsolete by April 1917, and more than 70 B.E.2s would fall to German pilots that month. (Mirrorpix via Getty Images)

The Halberstadt CL.II 1917 had a 160hp engine and top speed of 103mph. It carried a 50kg bombload and was armed with two machine guns. From summer 1917, it was one of the main aircraft equipping the Schlachtstaffel. (AC)

Breguet 14 bombers on an airfield during the winter of 1917. The Breguet began to equip the French bomber force in summer 1917. Its use of a metal frame made it very sturdy and easier to mass produce. With a 300hp engine (some versions had up to 400hp engines), its top speed was 121mph. Armed with three machine guns and carrying 355kg of bombs, it was a formidable bomber that equipped most French and many American bomber squadrons in 1918. (AC)

## Air services and aircraft production

From the first weeks of the war, all the Great Powers understood that a large, capable aviation arm was an invaluable asset. At the start of the war, aircraft became the major source of intelligence for all the combatants, and reconnaissance and observation would remain the primary mission for all the air services. By 1915, the establishing of large air forces to dominate the battlefield and ensure effective reconnaissance and artillery observation, while denying the same to the enemy, became a top priority.

The air war of World War I was, much like that on the ground, a function of numbers. The two leading nations of the Allies, Britain and France, worked together as an effective coalition from the very start of the war, sharing aircraft designs and engine manufacture, each ally allowing their partner full access to license the best engines and aircraft types available.

The creation of vast aircraft industries capable of mass-producing thousands of aircraft was a challenge that stretched the engineering capabilities of the major powers. France and Germany began the war with numerous aircraft manufacturers and sizeable aircraft engine industries. Britain had a much smaller aviation and engine manufacturing base, and would have to create a large engine and airframe industry almost from scratch.

Starting with larger aircraft and motor industries, France was able to maintain its production advantage during the war. Indeed, it was the French aircraft and engine industries that ensured Allied aerial superiority. From 1914–18, France manufactured 51,700 aircraft and a remarkable 92,386 aircraft engines. Germany's total production was 44,000 aircraft and 41,000 engines. After a huge effort, Britain surpassed

France in aircraft production late in the war, with an eventual wartime production of 55,092 aircraft and 41,034 engines. However, from 1914–17, the RFC relied heavily on purchasing French airplanes and engines. France supplied its allies with 9,800 aircraft and 24,550 engines. Almost all the aircraft that allowed the Americans to field a force of 750 front aircraft in 1918 were bought from France, including first-rate models such as the SPAD XIII, Bréguet 14 and Salmson 2A.

France's production superiority was due to greater industrial efficiency. Before the war, French car and engine manufacturers had already adopted the new American mass production techniques that culminated with Henry Ford's moving assembly line in 1913. With large factories carefully laid out to maximize the flow of materials, the French were able to use huge numbers of unskilled workers, including many women recruited to the war industries, to operate precision machines. The German aircraft and engine manufacturers relied more on hand-made techniques using skilled labour and did not adopt mass production methods until the last year of the war. The German and French aircraft industries each employed about 200,000 workers, but French worker productivity was much higher. In 1918, Britain's aircraft production slightly surpassed France's, but Britain employed a massive 375,000 workers in the aircraft industry. By concentrating on just a few aircraft models from 1917, France and Britain were able to produce large numbers of the selected models, with 7,000 SPAD XIIIs, 3,500 Bréguet 14s and 5,500 Sopwith Camels produced in 1917 and 1918. Only a few German models, such as the Fokker D.VII and the LVG and DFW two-seaters, ever cracked the 2,000 mark. What also hindered Germany was the excessive number of prototypes built (610) and aircraft models put into production (over 200), usually in small batches of a few hundred. In the end, quantity and decent quality trumped the smaller number of fine German airplanes. The Germans were always outnumbered by a factor of two or three to one in the air from 1917–18.

## Aircraft attrition – the problem of quality control

Although the French, and later the British and Germans, managed to develop mass-production techniques, all the Great Powers failed in terms of quality control for aircraft manufacture. In the rush to get new aircraft models to the front, it was normal for the aircraft in World War I to be proposed, designed, test-flown and put into production in a matter of just four or five months, from the concept drawings to the aircraft coming out of the factories. Rushed design and testing programmes resulted in many flawed aircraft designs, many of which were nonetheless placed into production, knowing that even a flawed new model was superior to the obsolete model of aircraft it was replacing.

Combat aviation went through several generations of aircraft between 1914 and 1918. Each new generation of fighter would establish dominance, only to become hopelessly obsolete a year later when the enemy fielded the next-generation fighter. Owing to the rapid development process, it was largely a matter of luck when a first-rate aircraft like the S.E.5 appeared at the front.

Engine failure was a common occurrence. The quality of French rotary engines was superior to their German copies, so the Germans salvaged French engines from shot-down planes to replace their own new factory engines. German in-line engines were more reliable than those of the Allies, with British-made engines being notoriously unreliable. The Hispano-Suiza 8-cylinder was generally a very good engine, but often, due to a design flaw in the oil feed, it would have a blockage that shut down the engine. It was not until the latter part of the war that the oil system was redesigned. Many airmen lost their lives when their engines quit on take-off and landing. Top British ace Captain James McCudden (57 victories) was killed

German Oberursel copy of a nine-cylinder French Le Rhône rotary engine. The rotary engine was used extensively by all powers during World War I because of its high power-to-weight ratio. Unlike liquid-cooled in-line engines, which turned a crankshaft very much like an auto engine, the entire rotary engine would spin, thus turning a propeller that was directly attached. While the rotary engine was efficient for the small and light airplanes of World War I, it was an aeronautical dead end. Rotary engines over 150hp produced too much torque, which made it hard for the pilot to control the aircraft. Rotary engines also lacked good throttle control. French Le Rhône and Clerget engines dominated the wartime rotary engine design, with German rotaries being derivative. (IWM Q 71652)

in July 1918 when his engine failed just after he took off, forcing him to crash into the trees at the end of the runway.

Many of the best aircraft of the war had design problems that often made them deadly for their pilots. When the German Albatros D.III arrived at the front in January 1917, it was regarded as a superb aircraft. However, the sesquiplane configuration on the Albatros D.III used a new spar design for the lower wing which often cracked or broke during combat manoeuvres. A broken wing spar could result in a catastrophic breakup of the aircraft and certain death. However, in many cases, a crippled aircraft could be nursed down to a landing on the ground. This happened once to Freiherr von Richthofen, who barely regained control before making a crash landing. A pilot of Jasta 11, Vizefeldwebel Fester, had this experience during the April 1917 fighting, surviving a controlled crash. The Albatros wing spar was redesigned several times, and aircraft were recalled for modifications. Yet the problems with

An early version of the twin-engine Caudron G.4 bomber, with the open-boom tail assembly. In early 1917 it was a mainstay of the French reconnaissance force at Chemin des Dames. The G.4 was obsolete and was being replaced with the larger-engined Caudron G.6, which was beginning to arrive in the French squadrons. (SeM/Universal Images Group via Getty Images)

the wing spar failure persisted in the Albatros D.III and D.V. Interestingly, the similar Pfalz D.III never had this problem. However, the Albatros D.III was so effective in combat that the pilots flew it regardless of the dangers.

A common design problem on the Nieuport fighters was a tendency for the fabric of the upper wing to shred, requiring the pilot to make an immediate emergency landing before it could cause the complete breakup of the aircraft. Despite attempts to solve the flaw, problems with the Nieuport upper wing persisted and resulted in many deaths. The hastily designed iconic Fokker Dr.I triplane had the same problem, which led to the death of several pilots, and it had to be grounded in autumn 1917 while the aircraft were modified.

It was difficult to design a landing gear that could manage the weight of a heavy aircraft such as the German Gotha G.IV bomber or the French Bréguet 14. More Gothas were written off to landing accidents than to combat. French and American squadrons issued the Bréguet 14 had to modify and rebuild the landing gear before the aircraft could be flown.

Throughout the war, the aircraft and aircrew attrition rate to operational accidents equalled or exceeded the losses to combat. This was certainly the case for the French Air Service in the Nivelle Offensive, when it lost more aircraft and aircrew to accidents than to German fighters or flak. This latter situation was caused by awful weather – with snow, icing and high winds – that prevailed on the Chemin des Dames sector. Major combat operations required aircraft to fly in marginal conditions.

Histories of the air war of 1914–18 carefully detail combat and combat claims and losses, but figures on the high level of non-combat aviation losses are more difficult to ascertain. Even though thousands of aircraft were being produced every month in 1917–1918, it still took considerable time to increase the air units on the front due to enormous attrition rates caused by operational accidents and maintenance problems. On any day, the official number of aircraft in front units of the Allied or German air services had about 30 per cent of their total unserviceable.

A French Farman F.40 pusher biplane. The Farman F.40, designed in 1915, served as both a bomber and a reconnaissance plane. Though slow and underpowered, it was still serving in many French observation squadrons in spring 1917. (Galerie Bilderwelt/Getty Images)

**OPPOSITE** STANDARD AIR FORMATIONS AND MANOEUVRES, 1917

## Training for the air services

France and Germany established military air services in 1909 and quickly built considerable aviation forces prior to the war. Both nations realized that military flying required extensive and specialized training programmes, so military flight schools and observer courses were established before the war. Pilot and observer training lasted from three to six months.

After the war began, both France and Germany established a more extensive training curriculum and specialized schools. French pilots gained their basic pilot wings and were then sent to advanced courses before being transferred to combat units. Fighter pilots had to complete courses in advanced flying and gunnery before entering combat. In 1916, the Germans set up an advanced fighter course at Valenciennes, where the pilots (usually experienced pilots from observer units) were taught aerial combat by veteran fighter pilots. France and Germany also set up special courses for bomber and observation pilots.

The Germans established several schools for the advanced training of artillery and reconnaissance pilots. The Germans located one school for artillery pilots and observers in Kurland, in German-occupied Latvia, near the Russian north-western front. The Germans found that portion of the Eastern Front to be an ideal location for ultra-realistic training of their aviators, as the very weak Russian Air Service posed little threat to German pilots and the Russians had little in the way of anti-aircraft defences. Well above the range of Russian ground fire, German artillery pilots and observers in training would fly actual missions, directing German artillery batteries to fire upon identified Russian targets.

By 1916, the French and Germans had very systematic pilot and observer training, using trainers with dual controls and progressively working pilots up from basic trainers to current combat aircraft. New French and German pilots would arrive at combat units with an average of 90–100 flight hours. French and German squadrons had their own training for new pilots.

The RFC, established three years after the German and French air services and being a small service at the start of the war, had not developed similar training programmes. From 1914–16, aircrew training in the RFC was haphazard at best. Yet the need for additional pilots for the RFC was so intense that in spring 1917, British pilots with only 35 flight hours were being sent forward as replacements to the British fighter, reconnaissance and artillery flying units at the front. Experienced pilots who had survived a year or two of combat remarked that the new pilots barely knew how to fly their own aircraft, much less engage in combat.

The French and German air services lost about a quarter of their total aircrew casualties during the war in training accidents. In contrast, the British suffered almost half of their total fatalities from training accidents. Only in 1917, after appeals from General Trenchard, did the RFC make an effort to revise and improve the pilot training and establish proper courses for air observers, who were usually artillery officers who had volunteered and been given some training on the front. As RFC training improved with more dual-seat instruction and a longer programme, the training accident losses dropped by half, and by late 1917 British replacement pilots arrived at the front much better trained than before.

In the aftermath of the air combat over Arras in spring 1917, the RFC had finally understood that their pilot training programme needed to be completely revised. Indeed, some of Britain's top pilots, such as the ace Captain James McCudden, were sent back for a short tour of duty in Britain to help train new pilots. In 1917, the training programme was lengthened and a more extensive curriculum was instituted, including dual-seat instruction. By late 1917, British replacement pilots appeared at the front as well-trained as their German

Diving attack

Fokker Bounce

Reverse

Immelmann Turn

Squadron echelon-formation

V-formation

opponents. However, the training reforms came too late for the RFC in April 1917, which suffered high losses in combat against much better trained enemies.

## Fighter tactics

With the development of the fighter arm in 1915, the French, German and British fighter unit commanders soon developed tactics to shoot down enemy aircraft. Captain Oswald Boelcke, one of Germany's first fighter aces, drew up a summary of principles for fighter contact in summer 1916. Boelcke's tactics soon became the norm for Allied pilots too.

Boelcke's first principle was for the pilot to secure every advantage before initiating an attack. Whenever possible, the pilot was to keep the sun behind him when making an attack and thereby gain the element of surprise. Pilots should also use a speed advantage, which further increased the chance of taking an enemy by surprise. An aircraft with a 10–20mph higher speed had an advantage in the ability both to initiate combat action and to break off that action. One way to gain a speed advantage was to use the wind. It was common practice in 1917 for German squadron commanders to carefully study the daily meteorological reports from the Luftstreitkräfte's weather section. These reports provided estimated wind speeds at different altitudes. When planning an interception, a fighter squadron would move to an altitude where the wind favoured them, a tail wind increasing the speed of a diving aircraft.

Another principle of Boelcke was to understand the capabilities of one's own aircraft vis-à-vis the enemy plane. Some aircraft were faster than others, yet slower aircraft might be more manoeuvrable and therefore have an advantage in a clash at close quarters. One principle of Boelcke's, employed by nearly all the leading World War I aces, was to get as close as possible to the enemy aircraft before firing. The two machine guns on the Albatros were calibrated on a ground firing range to converge at 100m, as 100m or less was the preferred range for engaging an opponent. A further principle was not to run away from one's attacker, which would leave the attacker on one's tail, but rather to turn in to the attacker. This would throw off the attacker's aim and allow the defending fighter an opportunity to manoeuvre and gain the initiative.

Boelcke recommended that fighters initiate attacks in flights of between four and six aircraft. As soon as combat was joined, however, each attacking fighter pilot was to single out one enemy aircraft for destruction. Boelcke recommended against two aircraft ganging up on one, since the close manoeuvring space of the era led to a high risk of mid-air collision. These tactics were based on the reality of aerial combat. Two different airplanes moving at 90–120mph and manoeuvring made it difficult to hit a moving target, so achieving surprise became key.

Jasta 11's Albatros D.III fighters lined up at Douai Airfield in April 1917. Jasta 11 was the top German fighter squadron in April 1917, with 89 confirmed victories. (AC)

### Rear attack and Fokker Bounce

The best and simplest manoeuvre to ensure an aerial victory was for a fighter pilot to get behind an enemy aircraft and shoot from close range. One of the most effective ways to shoot down an enemy pilot was called the 'Fokker Bounce'. In this manoeuvre, the attacking fighter dived down behind and then below

an enemy aircraft, then climbed to fire his guns into the enemy from behind and beneath. A competent fighter pilot constantly looked to the rear, but most pilots did not look behind and below the aircraft, so the Fokker Bounce provided the best way to take an enemy unawares. However, to achieve victory with the Bounce, the attacking pilot needed to be an exceptionally good marksman, because it required him to maintain his aiming point ahead of the enemy aircraft so that the enemy would fly into the fire. A competent defending pilot could therefore evade an attack from behind or below simply by turning his aircraft sharply. By turning or throttling back and slowing his speed, the former defender would become the attacker in a firing position behind the former attacker.

A flight of SE 5a aircraft in V-Formation, the normal formation for a flight of 3-6 aircraft.(Alamy)

## The Immelmann Turn

One of Germany's first great fighter aces, Captain Max Immelmann, invented a simple dogfight manoeuvre in 1916. To execute what became known as the Immelmann Turn, the pilot would first pull up very hard, and then wing over and drop altitude quickly. This manoeuvre could put a fighter plane on the tail of an erstwhile attacker, or else he could turn at a 90-degree angle to break combat. The French promoted a similar manoeuvre, with a hard climb at the beginning of a loop. At the top of the loop, the pilot would simply roll the aircraft right-side-up, ending up at a higher altitude and flying in the opposite direction.

Another way to break combat was to put one's aircraft into a spin. A spin occurs when the aircraft has an angle of attack so high that the aircraft's forward movement simply stalls, as if applying the brakes. When an aircraft stalls, it will wing over and start spinning, pointing directly at the ground. In a spin, one loses altitude very quickly. Up until 1916, it was believed that spins were irreversible and meant an inevitable death. However, it was discovered by both Allied and German pilots that recovering from a spin was actually simple. When an aircraft went into a spin, the pilot needed only to push the stick forward all the way and then pull the stick back all the way while applying firm pressure to the rudder in the opposite direction of the aircraft's spin. This ended the spin and had the aircraft flying straight and

Rittmeister Manfred von Richthofen, Commander of Jasta 11, the highest-scoring fighter unit in the campaign (with 89 victories). Von Richthofen was not only Germany's top ace, with 80 victories, but was also a brilliant leader who trained and mentored his pilots. (AC)

level again. The pilot's main consideration for initiating a spin was that he needed plenty of altitude, because an aircraft could easily drop a thousand feet in a few seconds before he could recover. A spin was a useful ruse for any pilot finding himself at a disadvantage, and hundreds of aircraft were reported as fighter kills when witnesses noted the plane spinning out of control and out of the fight, when in reality the aircraft and pilot lived to fight another day. Because the spin was such a good a defensive tactic, Boelcke insisted that the fighter pilot follow a seemingly disabled aircraft all the way down.

## Squadron tactics
### V-formation

In 1916, flying either with an entire squadron of between ten and 15 aircraft or in a flight of four or five aircraft became the norm for fighter operations. Both the Allies and the Germans developed an array of standard fighter unit tactics in order to allow the most effective fighting. In a flight or squadron formation, as aircraft did not have radios and could not communicate, the simplest formation was based on a 'V', with the flight or squadron leader at the tip of the 'V'. In this case, the aircraft of the flight or squadron would simply follow their commander. In flight or squadron tactics, it was the commander who chose the moment, the altitude and the spot to initiate combat.

### Echelon (group formation)

Two to four flights might be combined in a squadron or group formation, all following the lead of the squadron commander. The simplest and most common formation was the echelon, in which the lead flight would be in the lowest position, with the squadron commander at the front of the 'V'. Echeloned behind and above the squadron commander were additional flights, all in a position to observe the squadron commander's movements and to follow his lead. As Commander of Jasta 11, Rittmeister Manfred von Richthofen commonly flew with two flights. Later in 1917, more than one squadron might fly on a mission: there might be two or three flights echelon-stacked behind and above the squadron or group commander, all following his lead.

It was the squadron commander flying in front who would pick the target and initiate an attack. At this point, once combat was begun, it was every pilot for himself. Diving on an enemy, each pilot would single out and concentrate on a single aircraft. As the squadron commander, von Richthofen followed the guidelines of Captain Boelcke, who had been his mentor when von Richthofen first joined the fighter force. He would initiate combat only when he could gain the most favourable advantage. For example, on more than one occasion von Richthofen, spotting a British bomber mission, allowed the British squadron to conduct their mission while he took Jasta 11 to a higher altitude and waited for the British squadron to return. Then, diving out of the sun, with a tail wind to provide extra speed, von Richthofen would put his entire squadron into a surprise attack. It was this kind of careful consideration, as well as von Richthofen's diligent mentoring and training of all his pilots, which gave Jasta 11 such a stellar performance in spring 1917.

# CAMPAIGN OBJECTIVES
## The Nivelle Offensive

### The strategic situation in early 1917

In winter 1916–17, the German Supreme High Command determined a new war strategy for 1917. On the Western Front, the Germans had 154 divisions facing 190 French, British and Belgian divisions, so their armies would assume the defensive. On the Eastern Front, meanwhile, where the Germans had enjoyed a series of major victories that had decimated the Russian Army, the Germans would exploit any favourable opportunities. Britain, seen as the financial and industrial centre of the Allies, would be attacked by unleashing unrestricted submarine warfare to blockade the economy and through an air campaign by heavy bombers that would serve as a psychological blow to the British public. The Germans hoped that these moves would bring the Allies to the negotiating table. The Supreme High Command was already building up a force of multi-engine Gotha G.IV and four-engine *Riesen* (Giant) bombers to be based in Flanders to begin the bombing campaign in the spring. The G.IV heavy bomber carried a 500kg bombload.

The Supreme High Command decided to strengthen the defensive line on the Western Front by building a new defence line with many concrete bunkers and concrete strongpoints to resist Allied artillery. The Germans called the defence line the Siegfriedstellung, but the Allies named it the 'Hindenburg Line'. To free up German divisions for a general reserve to counter the expected Allied offensives, a large salient south of Arras 120km long and 45km wide at its widest point (200km²) in the centre of the Western Front would be abandoned and the army would withdraw to a strong new defensive line that was carefully surveyed to take advantage of the terrain. This would shorten the front line by 50km and free up 13 divisions for the general reserve.

### New defensive doctrine

Hindenburg and Ludendorff rejected the defensive doctrine used in the Somme battles that emphasized holding the front line at all costs. In late 1916, the concept of 'elastic defence'

French 155mm howitzer. France started the war with few heavy guns, but by 1917 the French artillery force fielded thousands of guns over 100mm in calibre. This howitzer, with a range of over 16km, was especially important for counter-battery fire. (Photo 12/Alamy Stock Photo)

**OPPOSITE** GERMAN DEFENSIVE AIR DOCTRINE, 1917

was introduced: the creation of three defensive lines, with the first line lightly held and the second line, 2–3km to the rear, being the main defence barrier. A third and final defence line was established another 2–3km further back. Army reserves and reinforcement divisions would be located behind the second line, ready for immediate counter-attack if the first line was taken. The counter-attack forces would be supported by regimental-sized mobile artillery units with light and medium guns.

### The Allied strategic view

After the bloody and inconclusive 1916 campaigns, the French government lost confidence in commander-in-chief General Joffre. His steadiness had saved the French Army in the autumn of 1914. Now, however, he was seen as a tired old man lacking the strategic vision needed to decisively win the war. The French government believed what was needed was a general capable of carrying out a decisive offensive and breaking the Germans. Accordingly, Joffre was retired as army commander in December 1916. The government passed over army group commanders including Philippe Pétain and Ferdinand Foch in favour of an unusual pick: army commander General Robert Nivelle. Pétain, hero of Verdun, was regarded as too defensive-minded, lacking aggressiveness. Nivelle, on the other hand, had proven himself to be the most aggressive, offensive-minded army commander in the Verdun battles.

In October 1916, Nivelle had made himself a national hero by conducting a brilliant offensive against the Germans at Verdun, retaking Fort Douaumont and the high ground to the east that had been lost earlier in the year. Nivelle delivered a stinging defeat to the German Army, taking over 10,000 prisoners without excessive casualties. He was an artilleryman, and his expertise in artillery and in new tactics had been one of the few advantages for the French Army at Verdun. Nivelle carried out a short but intense artillery preparation with heavy guns, one of the most massive barrages of the war. It was especially devastating to the German rear

A German heavy howitzer, dug in behind the lines. Guns such as this one, firing heavy shells, were exceptionally lethal in breaking up attacks. (Alamy Stock Photo)

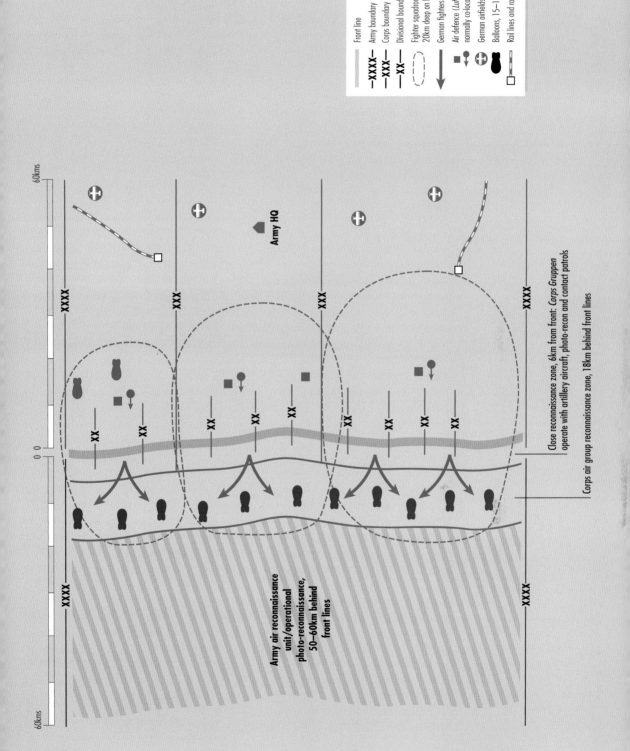

**Army air reconnaissance unit/operational photo-reconnaissance, 50–60km behind front lines**

Army HQ

Close reconnaissance zone, 6km from front: *Corps Gruppen* operate with artillery aircraft, photo-recon and contact patrols

Corps air group reconnaissance zone, 18km behind front lines

60kms

0

60kms

—XXXX—
—XXX—
—XX—

**Key**

| | |
|---|---|
| | Front line |
| —XXXX— | Army boundary |
| —XXX— | Corps boundary |
| —XX— | Divisional boundary |
| | Fighter squadron operations area, 20km deep on both sides of the front |
| | German fighters attack Allied balloons |
| | Air defence (*Luftschutz*) officers/detachment, normally co-located with flak platoons |
| | German airfields |
| | Balloons, 15–16km behind front |
| | Rail lines and railhead |

The Salmson 2A, first fielded in 1917, had a 231hp engine that brought it a top speed of 117mph. Its superior performance (its ceiling was 20,000ft) made it an excellent platform for aerial reconnaissance and artillery spotting. It was armed with one forward machine gun, and the observer had two machine guns in a twin mount. Given its speed and armament, it could survive on the battlefield. It was France's main observation plane in 1918. (adoc-photos/Getty Images)

areas now that the French had a large number of long-range heavy artillery pieces. Nivelle concentrated masses of French airpower and established such strong aerial superiority that the Germans were driven from the skies. Both during the preparatory phase and the attack itself, the German Army was relentlessly bombed and strafed by French bombers and fighters.

Meanwhile, French artillery flyers operated effectively, bringing heavy guns to bear against the Germans. For the initial advance, Nivelle employed a creeping barrage tactic in which the guns of an entire division or corps laid straight lines of fire in front of the German positions in no man's land, moving forward 100m every three minutes. At the Somme, the British artillery support had pounded the German front positions but then allowed them several minutes to leave their dugouts and return to their trenches and bunkers to man machine guns and artillery before the infantry attacked. Instead, the creeping barrage, with the artillery slowly 'walking' forward and the infantry advancing 100yds behind, rolled over the German-forward positions without giving the defenders time to emerge from their bomb-proof dugouts and man the defences. Nivelle maintained that his techniques of overwhelming airpower, improved air–ground artillery coordination techniques and the creeping barrage could be expanded to use on a larger scale.

France had by now developed a tank. By spring 1917, more than 150 tanks would be available, which Nivelle wanted to add as an important breakthrough weapon. It was Nivelle's enthusiasm for the potential use of new weapons and tactics that led to his elevation to the French High Command. Additionally, Nivelle was an asset for working with the BEF, for he had an English mother and spoke perfect English.

### Genesis of the Nivelle Plan

Shortly after taking over as Army Chief in January 1917, General Nivelle put his staff to work developing a grand plan for a combined French–British offensive that would break the German defences and, in one grand stroke, so cripple the German Army that Germany would be forced to sue for peace. Nivelle's concept was to have a French army group attack the south-eastern flank of the German salient at the centre of the Western Front. Simultaneously, the British would employ an army group to attack the northern flank of the salient at Arras. The plan would require masses of artillery, especially heavy guns, in a preparatory barrage that would exceed even the massive use of artillery at the Somme. Nivelle planned to use the same techniques that he had employed in a smaller army-sized attack at Verdun, but on a grand scale, with a breakthrough on both flanks of the salient. The British Army would turn south, and after its breakthrough, the French Army would turn north. They would then meet behind the German lines near St Quentin, cutting off and enveloping the German armies occupying the centre of the front.

Nivelle's plan included massing French aviation forces and the RFC in their respective sectors to win air superiority. In addition to artillery firepower, both the British and French would use tanks to shield their advancing infantry and crush the German barbed wire and forward defences. Nivelle passionately believed that he could end the war with this one short, grand campaign. As at Verdun, he anticipated achieving a breakthrough without excessive losses.

While the concept was ambitious, the terrain selected for the breakthrough featured powerful, well-manned German positions. Just east of Rheims, the French faced the high ridgeline of the Chemin des Dames, stretching for 40km and overlooking the valley of the River Aisne. For centuries, the French had quarried limestone on a large scale at the Chemin des Dames, creating cliffs over 200 metres high in places. Stone quarries provided admirable protection for the German troops, who had tunnelled into the Chemin des Dames and established large underground shelters and supply points for their troops that were impervious to all but the heaviest of the Allied guns. On the British sector, the Douai Plain was dominated by Vimy Ridge, not as long or as impressive a feature as the Chemin des Dames but one which had to be taken because it dominated the landscape for a large area, providing a superb position for artillery observation.

Nivelle, using his Verdun success as his model, failed to note significant differences. Before his October attack at Verdun, the Germans had already stripped the sector of several divisions and much of the supporting artillery, diverted to bolster the German Army's defence on the Somme. The Germans had also removed most of the air units from around Verdun to reinforce their units in the Somme battles. When Nivelle attacked at Verdun, the Germans thus lacked the means to carry out counter-attacks.

In meetings in January and February 1917, Nivelle briefed the British leaders on his concept for the grand offensive. General Sir Douglas Haig, commander of the BEF, held a sceptical view of Nivelle's plan. Haig instead wanted the priority of the BEF to be an offensive in Flanders, where he hoped to take the ground at Messines Ridge and at Ypres, the scene of the BEF's bloody battles of 1915. Haig intended to break through the Germans on their extreme right flank, at Flanders and along the Channel coast, then advance on to the Belgian plain.

At a strategy conference of the French and British staffs, held from 26–28 February, Nivelle laid out his plan in great detail, emphasizing the new artillery tactics, coordination methods and use of tanks that would bring a great Allied victory. Despite considerable scepticism on the British side, and also from French senior commanders, Nivelle's plan appealed to the political leaders and was adopted as the Allied strategy. The British Army would attack in the area of Arras in early April, then the French would attack in the Aisne Valley and Chemin des Dames immediately afterwards. The initial British attack and the supporting attack by a French army would draw off some of the German reserves and enable the French attack to succeed.

Aerial photography was also a key source for strategic intelligence. Photo observation craft flew deep behind enemy lines to photograph activity in the rear, with enemy rail traffic and logistics movement monitored and analyzed. This is a German photograph of Le Havre's port, taken at 19,000ft in 1917.(AC)

**OPPOSITE** BRITISH/FRENCH OFFENSIVE AIR DOCTRINE, 1917

Nivelle's belief that he could end the war with one quick, grand stroke was not shared by his own senior commanders. General Joseph Micheler, commander of the newly created Reserve Army Group of three armies that would make the main attack on the 40km front, refused to make any predictions for success. Nivelle's plan called for a complete breakthrough of the German defence lines in three days by the 5th and 6th armies, with the 10th Army to follow on in pursuit of the broken German forces. General Micheler doubted that the Germans would be as cooperative as they had been at Verdun the previous autumn, also noting that the terrain to be attacked was extremely defensible.

The 4th Army, belonging to General Pétain's Army Group Centre, would attack the southern flank of the Chemin des Dames held by the German 1st Army a day after the Reserve Army Group began its attack. The 10th Army under General Denis Duchêne would act as the follow-on force to exploit the breakthrough in the 5th and 6th army sectors. Nivelle held that an advance of 12–15km on the first day was possible, although, even under the best of conditions, a 7–8km advance was more likely. The French plan was originally intended to begin on 10 April, only a day after the British Army's attack at Arras. However, due to logistics problems and the weather, the French attack was first postponed to the 14th and then the 16th.

For their part, the British carried out intensive preparations for attacking Vimy Ridge, including vast tunnelling operations from their lines up close to the ridge. The British had also improved their artillery technique, planning to use even heavier artillery barrages than employed at the Somme. Like the French, the British had added a large number of very heavy guns such as the 60-pdr howitzer, which it was envisaged would be effective in destroying German fortifications and have enough reach to also serve as counter-battery guns.

A weak spot that Haig and his RFC commander, General Hugh Trenchard, noted was the obsolescence of British aircraft, made apparent over the Somme in autumn 1916. Trenchard was, of course, committed to making a maximum effort to support the ground troops, but he also feared the heavy losses against the new German fighter force, equipped with ever growing numbers of the Albatros D.IIIs. Trenchard lobbied London to get the new two-seater Bristol to the front as well as the R.E.8 observation planes and the new S.E.5 fighter.

# ORDER OF BATTLE: BRITISH, FRENCH AND GERMAN ARMY AND AVIATION FORCES IN THE NIVELLE OFFENSIVE

**ARRAS SECTOR: BRITISH AND GERMAN ORDER OF BATTLE, 9 APRIL 1917**
**BRITISH (ARRAYED NORTH TO SOUTH)**
**1st Army (General Henry Horne): eight divisions committed 9 April**
I Corps: 31st, 6th, 24th Divisions
Canadian Corps: 1st, 2nd, 3rd, 4th Canadian Divisions, 5th Division (British) in reserve
Aviation: RFC 1st Brigade – 144 aircraft
1st Wing: Squadrons No. 2, 5, 10, 16 (B.E.2s. Corps squadrons)

10th Wing: No. 25, 40, 43, 8 RNAS (25,F.E.2s; 40, Nieuports; 43, Sopwith Strutters; 8 RNAS, Nieuports)
No. 1 Balloon Wing. Three companies: 12 balloons
Air park
**British 3rd Army (General Edmund Allenby): 22 divisions**
XVII Corps: 9th, 51st, 34th, 4th, 39th Divisions
VI Corps (south of Scarpe) 2nd, 15th, 37th, 12th, 3rd Divisions
Exploitation Force: 1st, 3rd Cavalry Divisions.
VII Corps: 14th, 56th, 30th, 21st, 33rd Divisions

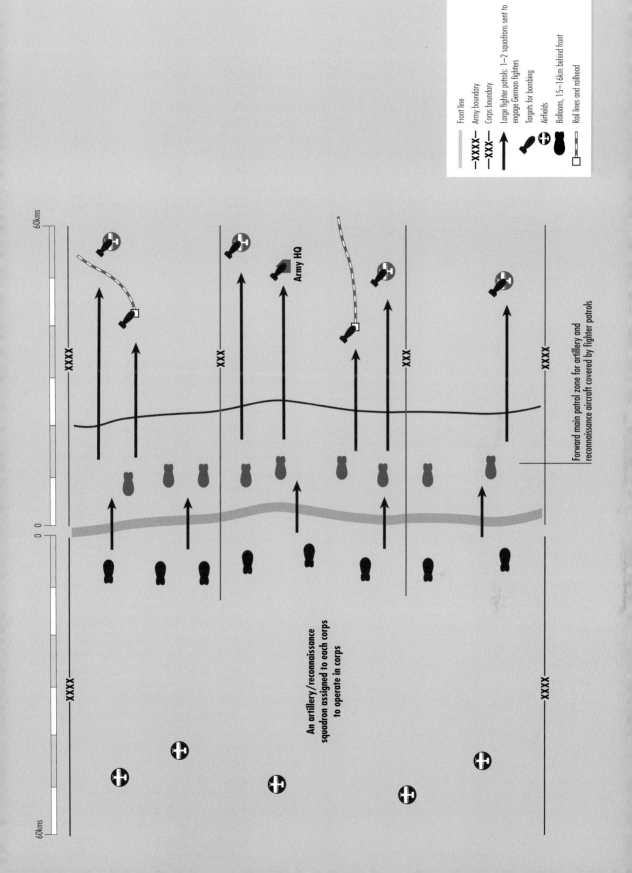

60kms

60kms

XXXX

XXXX

XXX

XXX

XXXX

XXXX

Army HQ

An artillery/reconnaissance squadron assigned to each corps to operate in corps

Forward main patrol zone for artillery and reconnaissance aircraft covered by fighter patrols

Front line

XXXX Army boundary

XXX Corps boundary

Large fighter patrols: 1–2 squadrons sent to engage German fighters

Targets for bombing

Airfields

Balloons, 15–16km behind front

Rail lines and railhead

Army Reserve: XIII Corps: 17th, 63rd Divisions north of Scarpe; 29th, 50th, 18th Divisions south of Scarpe

**Aviation: RFC 3rd Brigade – 198 aircraft**

12th Wing: Squadrons No. 8, 12, 13, 59 (Corps Squadrons: No. 8, 12, 13, B.E.2s; No. 59, R.E.8s)
13th Wing: Squadrons No. 11, 29, 48, 60, 100, 1 RNAS (No. 11, F.E.2s; 29, Nieuports; 48, Bristol F.2As; 60, Nieuports; 100, F.E.2s; 1 RNAS, Sopwith Triplanes)
Attached Cavalry Corps: No. 35 Squadron (AW F.K.8s)
No. 3 Balloon Wing: four companies, 16 balloons
Air park

**British 5th Army (General Hubert Gough): four divisions committed**

North Flank (supporting attack)
V Corps: Australian 4th Division, 62nd Division, 4th Cavalry Division, 7th Division

**Aviation: RFC 5th Brigade – 126 aircraft**

15th Wing: Squadrons No. 3, 4, 15 (Corps Squadrons), No. 3, Morane Parasols; 4, B.E.2s; 15, B.E.2s)
22nd Wing: Squadrons No. 18, 23, 32, 3 RNAS (No. 18, F.E.2s; 23, F.E.2s, SPAD VIIs; 32, DH.2s; 3 RNAS, Sopwith Pups)
Balloon Wing: four companies, 16 balloons
Air park

**GERMAN 6TH ARMY (GENERALOBERST LUDWIG VON FALKENHAUSEN): 16 DIVISIONS**

Ten Divisions in line, six in reserve/reinforcing. A further three divisions arrive by 10 April, bringing total strength of 6th Army to 19 divisions

**Gruppe Souchez** (VIII Reserve Korps): 56.Infanterie-Division, 80.Reserve-Division, 16.Bavarian Infanterie-Division, 4.Garde Infanterie-Division (relieving division)
**Gruppe Vimy** (Bavarian I Reserve Korps): 79.Reserve-Division, 1.Bavarian Reserve-Division, 14.Bavarian Infanterie-Division
Arriving: 111.Infanterie-Division, 1.Garde Reserve-Division. In rear: 3.Bavarian Infanterie-Division
**Gruppe Arras** (IX Reserve Korps): 11.Infanterie-Division, 17.Reserve-Division, 18.Reserve-Division, 220.Infanterie-Division. Relief: 18.Infanterie-Division, 17.Infanterie-Division
**German 6th Army Artillery**: 508 Field- und 323 heavy guns
**6th Army Aviation (Hauptmann Maximilian Sorg) – 210 aircraft**
Five Group headquarters
17 Observation/Artillery flights
Six Jasta
Six Schutzstaffel (Jasta 2, 5, 3, 8, 11, 33) plus Jastas 12 and 33 after 11 April
Balloon Detachments: 14 balloons

Reinforcements added, 11 April: 96 aircraft
Three Observation/Artillery flights – 18 aircraft
Two Jastas – 12 aircraft
Three Schutzstaffel – 18 aircraft
Five balloons

**CHEMIN DES DAMES SECTOR: FRENCH AND GERMAN ORDER OF BATTLE, 16 APRIL 1917**
**FRENCH ARMY AND AIR SERVICE**
**Groupe d'armées de Reserve (Reserve Army Group) 15 April 1917 – Commander, General Joseph Alfred Micheler**
**Aviation for Army Group:**
Three Fighter Groupes de Combat: 120 aircraft
**6th Army (Commander General Charles Mangin)**
VI Corps: 12e Division d'Infanterie, 56e Division d'Infanterie, 127e Division d'Infanterie
XI Corps: 21e Division d'Infanterie, 22e Division d'Infanterie
XX Corps: 11e Division d'Infanterie, 39e Division d'Infanterie, 153e Division d'Infanterie, 168e Division d'Infanterie
XXXVII Corps: 10e Division d'Infanterie, 158e Division d'Infanterie
I Colonial Corps: 2e Division d'Infanterie Colonial, 3e Division d'Infanterie Colonial
II Colonial Corps: 10e Division d'Infanterie Colonial, 15e Division d'Infanterie, e Division d'Infanterie Colonial
Independent divisions: 166e Division d'Infanterie, 97e Division d'Infanterie Territorial, 5e Division de Cavalerie
**6th Army Aviation**
Army Aviation Commander: one Fighter Escadrille, three Observation Escadrilles
Assigned to corps: 18 Escadrilles Artillery/Observation
16 balloons
Air park
220 aircraft
**10th Army (General Denis Auguste Duchêne)**
II Corps: 3e Division d'Infanterie, 4e Division d'Infanterie
III Corps: 5e Division d'Infanterie, 6e Division d'Infanterie, 130e Division d'Infanterie
IX Corps: 17e Division d'Infanterie, 18e Division d'Infanterie, 152e Division d'Infanterie
XVIII Corps: 35e Division d'Infanterie, 36e Division d'Infanterie
I Cavalry Corps: 1e Division de Cavalerie, 3e Division de Cavalerie
II Cavalry Corps: 2e Division de Cavalerie, 4e Division de Cavalerie, 7e Division de Cavalerie
Independent Division: 66e Division d'Infanterie

## 10th Army Aviation

Army Air Commander: one fighter Escadrille, three Observation Escadrilles
15 Observation/Artillery Escadrilles
12 balloons
Air park
190 aircraft

## 5th Army (General Olivier Mazel)
## Tank Groups: 128 tanks

I Corps: 1re Division d'Infanterie, 2e Division d'Infanterie, 51e Division d'Infanterie, 162e Division d'Infanterie, 4e Division d'Infanterie
II Corps: 40e Division d'Infanterie, 42e Division d'Infanterie, 69e Division d'Infanterie, 165e Division d'Infanterie
V Corps: 9e Division d'Infanterie, 10e Division d'Infanterie, 125e Division d'Infanterie
VII Corps: 14e Division d'Infanterie, 37e Division d'Infanterie, 41e Division d'Infanterie, 1re Brigade d'Infanterie Russe
XXXVIII Corps: 89e Division d'Infanterie Territorial, 151e Division d'Infanterie, 6e Division de Cavalerie
Army Reserve: 66e Division d'Infanterie, 3e Brigade d'Infanterie Russe

## 5th Army Aviation

Army Air Commander: one Fighter Escadrille, four Observation/Artillery Escadrilles
Corps Support: 16 Observation/Artillery Escadrilles
16 balloons
Air park
210 aircraft

## Army Group Centre – Supporting attack on southern flank of Chemin des Dames
## 4th Army (General Paul Anthoine)

VIII Corps: 16e Division d'Infanterie, 34e Division d'Infanterie, 128e Division d'Infanterie, 169e Division d'Infanterie
X Corps: 9e Division d'Infanterie, 2e Division d'Infanterie, 131e Division d'Infanterie
XII Corps: 25e Division d'Infanterie, 24e Division d'Infanterie, 60e Division d'Infanterie
XVII Corps: 33e Division d'Infanterie, 45e Division d'Infanterie, 15e Division d'Infanterie, 74e Division d'Infanterie, 55e Division d'Infanterie, 132e Division d'Infanterie

## 4th Army Aviation

Army Aviation Commander: one Fighter Escadrille, two Observation Escadrilles
1st GB (Bomber Group): 40 aircraft
Corps Support: 12 Observation/Artillery Escadrilles
Air park
12 balloons
200 aircraft

## GERMAN ARMY AND AIR, APRIL 1917
## German 7th Army (General Max von Boehn)
## 16 April: 18 divisions

XX Reserve Corps: 46. Reserve-Division, 13.Landwehr-Division plus reinforcements: 2.Garde Infanterie-Division, 21.Reserve-Division
XI Corps: 211.Infanterie-Division, 222.Infanterie-Division, 25.Infanterie-Division, 183.Infanterie-Division plus reinforcements: 45.Reserve-Division
XV Bavarian Corps: 9.Bavarian Reserve-Division, 5.Bavarian Reserve-Division plus reinforcements: 213. Infanterie-Division
Gruppe Liesse: 16.Reserve-Division, 5.Garde-Division, 20.Infanterie-Division, 1.Garde Reserve-Division, 44.Reserve-Division plus reinforcements: 33.Reserve-Division

## 7th Army Aviation (Commander Hauptmann Walter Stahr)

Four Gruppe Headquarters
18 Flieger Abteilung (reconnaissance and artillery)
Eight Schutzstaffel
Six Jagdstaffel (Jastas 1, 13, 17, 19, 32) plus Jasta 35 after 17 April
Air park
202 aircraft
Reinforcements after 17 April: 24 aircraft
Jasta 35, two Artillery Flights

## German 1st Army (General Fritz von Below):
## 15 divisions

plus reinforcements: 215.Infanterie-Division, 58.Infanterie-Division, 30.Infanterie-Division, 5.Infanterie-Division
Gruppe Aisne: 21.Reserve-Division, 4.Infanterie-Division
Gruppe Brimont: 54.Infanterie-Division, 34.Infanterie-Division
Gruppe Reims: 19.Infanterie-Division, 7.Reserve-Division, 13.Reserve-Division, 14.Reserve-Division
Gruppe Prosnes: 29.Infanterie-Division, 214.Infanterie-Division, 6.Infanterie-Division

## 1st Army Aviation (Commander Hauptmann Wilhelm Haehnelt)

Four Gruppe Headquarters
15 Flieger Abteilungen (Reconnaissance and Artillery)
Ten Schutzstaffel
Five Jastas (Jastas 17, 19, 24, 29, 36)
192 aircraft

# THE CAMPAIGN
## Bloody April

### March 1917: Germans withdraw to the Siegfriedstellung

The Royal Aircraft Factory S.E.5a. was one of the great fighter planes of World War I. Introduced in the Arras Campaign in April 1917, the S.E.5's original 150hp engine gave it a maximum speed of 125mph. However, only 77 of this model were made and the definitive version, the S.E.5a, had a 200hp Wolseley Viper engine that gave it a top speed of 135mph. It was the first British fighter to be equipped with two forward-firing machine guns, a synchronized Vickers machine gun that fired through the propeller and a Lewis gun mounted on the top wing. More than 5,000 S.E.5s were produced during the war. (SSPL/Getty Images)

The German withdrawal from the large salient was named Operation *Alberich* and began in February, carried out in utmost secrecy, while German front units prepared to move to the Siegfriedstellung in late March. The whole operation was very systematic, the Germans destroying anything of military value in the area, moving the logistics to the rear and pulling out their troops by stages. The Supreme High Command feared that if the Allies observed the movement and attacked while the Germans were leaving the salient, it might prove disastrous.

Allied air observation did in fact note the German activity, and on 4 March 1917, General Franchet d'Esperey, commander of the French Northern Army Group, requested permission to attack immediately – perhaps the best idea of the entire Spring 1917 Campaign. Nivelle, focused on the preparations for his own plan, rejected d'Esperey's proposal. Once the Germans pulled into the Siefriedstellung unmolested, they were in a better position, with 13 extra divisions to meet the expected Allied offensive. With the salient gone, and with it the opportunity to cut off exposed German divisions, Nivelle refused to change the concept. The attack would proceed as planned, but instead of pincers against a salient, British and French armies would advance and envelop the German centre. Neither Nivelle nor Haig ever clearly coordinated with the responsible army commanders as to exactly how the follow-up troops would carry out a deep envelopment after the initial breakthrough.

### Preparing the Nivelle Offensive

Throughout the winter of 1916–17, both sides prepared for the expected Allied spring offensive. In the original Nivelle Offensive plan, General Nivelle had promised 'Nothing less than the total destruction of most of the enemy forces on the Western Front.' His new air commander, Commandant Paul de Peuty, had argued that 'Victory in the air is the prerequisite of victory on the ground', and he issued directives to the French Air Service fighter squadrons that their aim was to destroy the German fighter squadrons.

## Air operations prior to the offensive

The vast movement of troops, supplies and artillery pieces into the two Allied attack sectors, which began in March, did not go unnoticed by the Germans. In the Arras sector, German reconnaissance sent in regular reports on the increase in rail traffic and laying of new rail lines, the building of cantonments for an estimated 120,000 additional troops, new supply dumps and an energetic road-building campaign. The German Air Service also noted increased air activity of all types, including bombing raids, observation flights and fighter sweeps in both the British and French sectors. By 16 March, the German Supreme High Command knew approximately where the French and British would attack. The German 6th Army commander in the Arras sector, and the 7th and 1st armies that would also face the French, directed major improvements in their defences, each army allotted additional divisions as well as reinforcing divisions and mobile artillery groups that would be placed just behind the front in threatened sectors, ready to conduct immediate counter-attacks as per German doctrine.

For the airmen, the air campaign over Arras, which became known as 'Bloody April', actually began with intense combat over the Arras and Chemin des Dames fronts throughout March. The increased number of Allied aircraft alone was an indicator of where the expected Allied offensives would strike. The German 1st and 7th armies' aviation forces had been small, as their part of the front had long been a quiet sector. In March and early April, however, they were strongly reinforced with additional air group headquarters, Jastas, Schustas and artillery flights transferred from other armies. The 6th Army aviation force was also reinforced. When the battle began, more air units would be committed. The Germans also improved their extensive communications net. Consequently, both on the ground and in the air, the Germans were fully prepared to meet the Nivelle Offensive.

German trenches and dugouts behind the front line at the Chemin des Dames, spring 1917. A German artillery battery, probably in the third defensive line, is sheltering in deep trenches and deep dugouts capable of withstanding a heavy barrage. The Chemin des Dames was an exceptionally strong defensive position for the German 7th and 1st Armies. (Shotshop GmbH/Alamy)

# The French front

After a quiet winter, March saw vastly increased French air activity, primarily on the Chemin des Dames front. In March, the French Air Service suffered 148 air casualties, 84 from combat (49 killed and missing in action, 35 wounded) and the remaining 64 casualties (22 dead, 42 injured) from aircraft accidents. French reconnaissance increased along the front, and on 6 April the French began a massive nine-day preliminary artillery bombardment along the Chemin des Dames sector, which required artillery escadrilles to make a maximum effort, even in marginal weather. The French air commander, Commandant de Peuty, ordered that the Fighter Groupes de Combat be used en masse to conduct grand sweeps to clear the sky of all German fighter planes behind the front lines. This tactic had worked well to gain air superiority at Verdun a few months before. De Peuty believed that French fighter forces would destroy the German Jastas in mass attacks, and after the breakthrough, French fighters would fly deep behind the German lines to attack troop columns in the German rear area.

During the preparatory phase, de Peuty's fighter groups flew in massive formations up to 90km behind the German lines. On 5 and 7 April, formations of 20 SPAD VIIs flew deep into German lines yet encountered no enemy aircraft. De Peuty had counted upon the Germans flying their squadrons into the large French formations and being destroyed through superior numbers. The German 1st and 7th army air commanders simply declined to oblige the French and commit their Jastas to pointless attacks where the Germans would be at a disadvantage.

The Luftstreitkräfte's air defence teams monitored French air activity and the well-informed army and corps air group commanders deployed the Jastas where they would have the best advantage. Instead of engaging the French fighter sweeps in early April, the Germans concentrated on shooting down French observation planes and artillery spotters close to the front lines, realizing that these aircraft posed a far greater danger to the German Army than enemy fighters flying behind German lines.

The preferred German fighting method was to use a flight of three or four aircraft that would attain surprise and pounce upon the French artillery and reconnaissance planes, then speed away while avoiding any French escort fighters. In the week before the French attack at Chemin des Dames, the German fighter planes caused considerable damage to the French reconnaissance forces. The air group of the French II Colonial Corps, equipped with Caudrons and Farmans, lost 14 of their 33 aircraft between 10 and 16 April.

The French Letord Let.1 three-seat, twin-engine reconnaissance biplane. The Letord was a fairly capable bomber and in early 1917, 300 were serving in the French Air Service, mostly in the reconnaissance squadrons. The Letord Let.1 was relatively fast at 98mph, but not very manoeuvrable. The French air commanders looked to replace the Letord with the Sopwith 1½ Strutter because the Letord was so large that it clogged up the French forward airfields. (IWM Q 67223)

Not all losses were due to German fighters, for the French suffered a high accident rate caused by flying in marginal weather, including thick overcast and snowstorms that created extremely difficult conditions. The tactics of grand fighter sweeps earned considerable resentment from the French reconnaissance and artillery airmen. The artillery spotters spent up to seven hours a day in the air conducting fire missions for the French artillery and photographing the front lines, and de Peuty's tactics did little to protect their aircraft. Rather than relying on the single fighter escadrille assigned to each army for reconnaissance escort, the commanders of the French reconnaissance groups preferred to use their own aircraft, sometimes armed with an extra machine gun, for protection.

The weather on both the Arras and Chemin des Dames fronts continued to be a major obstacle for the Allied air services. Both the British and French sent up aircraft in the unseasonably severe weather of late March and early April 1917. Flying in fog, overcast, snow showers and high winds ensured an extremely high accident rate for the Allied aircraft. Indeed, the French lost almost as many aircraft and airmen in accidents as they did in the heavy fighting of that April. In April, the French Air Service suffered 130 casualties in combat (25 killed, 46 missing and 59 wounded). However, even more aircrew became accident casualties, with 59 killed and 93 injured, and a total of 266 aircraft were lost to accidents.

## Attacking the balloons

In 1917, both offensive and defensive air operations called for the destruction of the opponent's observation balloons. This was one task that few pilots wished to carry out. Although shooting down a balloon counted as equivalent to claiming an aircraft, even the top aces of the war preferred to increase their victories by shooting down aircraft rather than balloons, for aircraft were a much easier proposition. Any German or Allied pilot could count on a tethered observation balloon to be surrounded by a ring of heavy machine guns, and usually light anti-aircraft guns as well. Moreover, the German and Allied pilots discovered that actually igniting a huge balloon filled with highly flammable hydrogen gas was a difficult proposition. The gas bags would not always catch fire – not even from incendiary bullets – and would merely suffer damage from machine-gun holes that could be easily repaired.

## French artillery flyers supporting the pre-attack bombardment, Chemin des Dames

Despite days of marginal flying weather, the French artillery flyers did exceptional work by bringing highly accurate fire on the German 7th and 1st armies' front lines and rear areas along the Chemin des Dames during the nine-day preliminary bombardment. On 11 April, the German XII Corps, east of Rheims on the Chemin des Dames, reported that French artillery flyers were bringing accurate destructive fire onto the front-line defences, while also directing long-range guns to target German artillery positions behind the front and stopping all supply movements to the front. The French flyers were so effective that the German artillery was unable to respond with counter-battery fire.

This scene depicts a mission by Captain Joseph Vuillemin, commander of Observation Escadrille C11, directing French artillery fire just behind the German XII Corps lines east of Rheims above St Matin l'Heureux, at 1400hrs on 11 April, 1917. Captain Vuillemin is flying a Letord Let.1 bomber modified for observation work. The radio transmitter's antenna was a wire deployed from the observer's cockpit with a lead weight to hold it steady; it was reeled out after take-off and reeled in before landing. Vuillemin was one of the top observation pilots of the French Army. An artillery officer who became a pilot in 1913, he flew hundreds of hours in the Verdun Campaign and Spring 1917 Campaign as escadrille commander. In April and May 1917, his unit was flying in support of the Reserve Army Group. Vuillemin was also known for his aggressiveness in attacking German observation planes he encountered. A month after this mission, he and his observer shot down a German observation plane while flying this aircraft.

His observer has just spotted in the distance a flight from Jasta 35, which was active in this sector to engage French observation flyers, but Vuillemin was able to evade the German fighters.

During April, each side carried out a consistent campaign to knock out the other's balloons. During March along the Chemin des Dames front, the Germans struck 14 of the French balloons, six of which caught fire and suffered total destruction, but the remaining eight were merely damaged. The balloon observers, who were highly trained artillery officers, suffered a high casualty rate in March, nine of the French balloon observers being killed or wounded during the attacks. The German assaults on the French balloons persisted in the first two weeks of April before the French attack. From 1–15 April, German fighters managed to set fire to seven French balloons and damage three more, inflicting seven casualties among the French balloon observers.

## The air campaign prior to the British attack

In terms of the aviation forces, the real campaign for Vimy Ridge and the Douai Plain began on 5 April, when there was some improvement in the weather. The British sent up all of their reconnaissance assets on 5 and 6 April to take some 1,700 aerial photographs of the German positions. German aerial resistance was also very heavy on those days.

The first combat use of the two-seater Bristol fighters took place on 5 April when a flight of six Bristols from No. 48 Squadron, led by Captain William Robinson VC, flew a patrol over the German lines. No. 48 Squadron was based 40km from the front, and their approach was spotted by Luftstreitkräfte ground observation teams, who reported the patrol to the Jastas. The Bristols were met by a flight of five aircraft from Jasta 11, led by Manfred von Richthofen. Instead of using their speed advantage and good manoeuvrability to engage the Germans with their forward-firing machine guns, Robinson signalled his Bristols to maintain a tight defensive formation. Diving from altitude, von Richthofen's flight picked their targets. Within minutes, they shot down four of the Bristols, including Captain Robinson, who was wounded and taken prisoner. Of the two Bristols that returned to their airfield, one was so badly shot up that it had to be scrapped.

In addition to the four Bristols, the British lost a Sopwith 1½ Strutter, a DH.2, two F.E.2Bs, two Martinsydes, two B.E.2s and five Nieuport 17s in the intense combat over the Arras sector that day. Although the RFC claimed more than a dozen German aircraft, the Germans had lost only one plane. The problem of over-claiming was a feature of the entire campaign. The excessive British claims included in the count any German aircraft seen diving

An LVG C.II two-seater corps reconnaissance plane. The boxy-looking LVG C.II and C.III and DFW two-seaters were the mainstays of the German photo and artillery flyer units in 1917 and 1918. With 180hp, they had a top speed of 102mph and good performance at higher altitudes. They were armed with one forward-firing machine gun, and another operated by the observer. The Germans had a significant advantage in their observation/artillery aircraft in spring 1917, as the LVGs and DFWs were superior to their French and British counterparts. (IWM)

away from the engagement as an aircraft out of control. Despite the heavy losses of the RFC, British air commanders remained convinced that they were causing heavy casualties to the Germans, which was certainly not the case. As most air combat took place over the German lines, the British had no way to accurately count aerial victories. On the other hand, German victory claims, while slightly exaggerated, tended to be fairly accurate because they were able to actually recover the downed aircraft lost in their territory.

The loss of five of the British Nieuports on 5 April was clear proof that the German Albatros D.IIIs outmatched the Nieuports that had dominated the skies over Verdun and in the first stage of the Somme Offensive. Intense combat continued on 6 April as the British continued their reconnaissance missions, which were bloodier than the previous day with 24 British aircraft shot down.

## The Arras sector: the RFC's bombing campaign

In the days leading up to the British attack, the RFC carried out a series of night bombing raids on German airfields across the front. The F.E.2s now served as night bombers as they stood little chance of survival in the fighter role. Dropping the RFC's standard 20lb light bombs, the F.E.2s would have to make their attacks at low levels, as accuracy at higher altitudes was impossible. Yet even at low altitude, the RFC's night attacks with small bombs proved inaccurate. Although the bomber pilots would report large fires and devastation after each raid, the reality is that the Germans suffered minimal damage from RFC bombing.

Jasta 11 experienced two night-time air raids by the RFC in the week before the attack began. Manfred von Richthofen remarked that 'maybe a rabbit might be terrified' by the British night bombing, but otherwise it had no effect on his unit's operations. Jasta 11 had taken a dozen captured enemy machine guns and built improvised wooden anti-aircraft mounts, manning them with Jasta 11's ground crew. During the second bombing raid, the German ground crew turned on a searchlight to illuminate the British aircraft, as any British pilot caught in the beam at low level would be briefly blinded. Von Richthofen also noted that the firing of machine guns stationed around the airfield had a great deterrent effect on British bombers, which then dropped their bombs haphazardly and flew home.

On 8 April, the RFC carried out a daylight bombing raid with the new DH.4 two-seater light bomber, also employed as an observation plane. A flight of six DH.4s from No. 55 Squadron crossed the front to bomb the German 6th Army Headquarters at Tournai, causing minor damage. On their return, the flight of DH.4s was ambushed by Jasta 11, which

## The S.E.5 proves its worth

While No. 56 Squadron was equipped with S.E.5s, Britain's top ace, flight commander Captain Albert Ball (with 30 aerial victories, mostly in a Nieuport), was sceptical about the new machine and was given permission to continue to fly his Nieuport 23 on lone patrols. On 23 April 1917, No. 56 Squadron began patrols with the S.E.5s. Because his Nieuport had been damaged in an early-morning encounter, Ball took up an S.E.5 (no. A4850) at 1130hrs and soon ran into a flight of Albatros D.IIIs. He downed one and managed to break contact with the rest using the S.E.5's superior speed. While returning to his airfield at 1230hrs, Ball encountered a lone Albatros C.III observation plane from Flieger Abt 7 near the front lines north of Cambrai.

In a diving attack Captain Ball put 40 rounds into the German machine, disabling it and wounding the observer. With a smoking engine, the German aircraft dived to the ground and managed to land. The German pilot and observer survived. Captain Ball now saw the worth of the S.E.5. Not only did the two machine guns give him extra firepower, but the speed advantage of the S.E.5 gave the pilot the initiative to initiate or break contact with enemy aircraft. Captain Ball would go on to shoot down 11 more German aircraft before his death in combat in May 1917.

lay in wait over Cambrai. German fighters shot down two of the DH.4s and a third was lost to German flak. The only notable British success that day was the destruction of two observation balloons by British fighters.

## The attack at Vimy Ridge and Arras, 9–14 April

The day before the British attack saw extremely harsh weather and little air combat. The British 1st and 3rd armies opened up the attack at Arras around midnight with a five-hour hurricane barrage designed to finish the destruction of the German front lines. All known German gun positions were especially targeted with a combination of high explosives and gas. The final pre-attack bombardment was extremely successful, as RFC air reconnaissance missions had identified 176 of 212 gun positions in the Vimy Ridge sector, so German defensive artillery fire was minimal that day.

Just after dawn, the four divisions of the 1st Army's Canadian corps went into battle for the first time as a single corps, with the objective of taking Vimy Ridge, defended by four German divisions. For weeks prior to the battle, the Canadian troops had rehearsed their attack in a training area behind the lines, and aerial photographs had been issued to the Canadian companies and battalions so that every officer and NCO could study their individual objectives.

Attacking on a 21km front, the British 1st and 3rd armies managed to create a far heavier and more focused bombardment than had been seen at the Somme. The preparatory bombardment was more effective now that the British used a greater proportion of heavy guns, with better shells and fuses. Along Vimy Ridge in the British 1st Army sector and the 3rd Army sector to the south, German front-line defences were largely obliterated, so the defenders were forced to shelter in their deep dugouts. Moreover, the Germans were short of ammunition and food, since the five days of preparatory bombardment had made it next to impossible to get provisions and supplies to the forward units.

British success on 9 April was due in part to the failure of the German 6th Army commander, General Ludwig von Falkenhausen, to follow the new defensive doctrine issued

The Rumpler C.IV, a two-seat German biplane specially designed for high-altitude operations. With a large upper wing and a modified high-compression, 240hp Maybach engine, the Rumpler C.IV had a ceiling of 20,000ft. In 1917, the observer was equipped with an automatic camera that, once activated, would take a high-resolution photograph every ten seconds. This way, a German observer could photograph several square kilometres of the front without having to load each photo plate. To operate in the extreme cold of high altitude, the pilot and observer wore electrically heated flight suits, and both used bottled oxygen to survive the thin air. Flying at 20,000ft, the Rumpler was above the ceiling of any Allied fighter aircraft or anti-aircraft gun. Built in small numbers, normally one Rumpler was assigned to each photo flight to be used for long-distance strategic observation. (AC)

A French aircraft parts factory near Paris. More than any other power, the French mastered the art of mass production of aircraft. The French carmakers, such as the Renault Company, had readily adopted production efficiency methodology and mass production methods developed first in America. French engine and aircraft companies like SPAD built aircraft in large factories using the latest-model machine tools and assembly-line techniques. The efficiency of French motor and aircraft manufacturers ensured that France produced far more engines and aircraft than Germany. French mass production enabled Allied air superiority for most of the war. The Allied powers of Russia, America, Britain and Italy used thousands of French-produced aircraft and engines during the war. (Alamy Stock Photo)

by the Supreme High Command early in the year. Von Falkenhausen ordered his divisions to hold the front line in force, rather than the second position. He also had the divisions sent by the Supreme High Command as reinforcements placed far to the rear, well away from any British artillery bombardment but also too far back to quickly counter-attack.

On the morning of 9 April, the advance of the 1st and 3rd British armies, behind a creeping barrage that moved forward 100 metres every three minutes, went very efficiently. North of the River Scarpe, the British XVII Corps employed 42 tanks in support, but these contributed little to the operation. By 0700hrs, the first German defence line had fallen, and the British had already moved up to attack the second defensive line by 0830hrs. The German defences at Vimy Ridge, the most important objective of the day, cracked quickly. German divisions there had been heavily decimated by the five days of preparatory bombardment, many German rifle companies reporting losses of 30–40 per cent before the attack began. Though the German troops on Vimy Ridge and in front of Arras fought fiercely, the well-trained Canadians were able to move through breaches in the first line of defence as they outflanked and encircled German strongpoints, forcing the defenders to surrender in batches of 100–200 men. By 1100hrs, the German lines were collapsing along the entire attack front. By afternoon, all units in the British offensive had achieved their objectives for that day. The shattered German defenders retreated, forming an improvised defence line at the third and final German defensive position.

Despite the overcast and poor visibility, the RFC was active that day in support of the ground troops. Behind Vimy Ridge, the German 42nd Field Artillery Regiment reported that low-flying British aircraft had strafed their positions, attacking anything that moved behind the ridge. Other German defenders of Vimy Ridge were also strafed by British planes.

Good intelligence and the highly effective use of artillery enabled the British 1st and 3rd armies to advance 6km in a single day, without excessive casualties. The British corps' fire plans had largely neutralized German defensive artillery fire. While the German infantry fought valiantly and fiercely, without effective artillery support they had no chance to hold the line, and 9 April saw the largest gain of ground on the Western Front since trench warfare had begun in late 1914. For the period 9–14 April, the Bavarian I Reserve Corps defending Vimy Ridge reported 10,500 casualties, as well as the loss of 120 artillery pieces including 42 heavy guns. The 100,000-man Canadian corps that attacked Vimy Ridge reported 11,000 casualties for the operation. The German Army in the Vimy sector alone lost upwards of 14,000 troops during the initial period of the campaign. This makes the British accomplishment at Vimy Ridge even more notable, in that the defenders took heavier losses than the attackers. By late afternoon on 9 April, with only moderate casualties and success all along the front, the British had created conditions for a breakthrough.

Too late, Von Falkenhausen had issued orders to bring up the reserve units, and they only arrived at the final defence line where the remnants of the front divisions were assembled on the night of 9 April. At that point, the Germans were only trying to organize a coherent defence and were in no position to conduct any counter-attacks. At the headquarters of the Supreme High Command, where Quartermaster General Erich von Ludendorff was celebrating his birthday, reports from the Arras sector came as a shock and provoked a crisis. Von Hindenburg ordered Colonel Fritz von Lossberg, known to be one of the German Army's top defensive specialists, to report immediately to the 6th Army Headquarters and take over as its chief of staff. Von Hindenburg gave von Lossberg orders that allowed him full command authority of the 6th Army, and if necessary he could override von Falkenhausen's orders. Two weeks later, von Falkenhausen was relieved of command and replaced with General Otto von Below. Von Falkenhausen was sent to be military governor of Belgium. The 72-year-old veteran of Prussia's 1866 and 1870 wars never again led combat troops.

Although the opportunity for a complete Allied breakthrough was possible, it was a fleeting chance. By late afternoon on 9 April, the British and Canadian troops had advanced to beyond supporting range of all but their heaviest artillery pieces. While Haig and his army commanders insisted upon moving forward to exploit the victory, the rain and snow had combined with the artillery preparation to reduce the entire front to muddy craters that made it difficult to move the British artillery and ammunition to new forward positions. The British delay in moving up supporting guns and supplies gave the German 6th Army time to sort itself out, prepare new defences and plan a counter-attack.

## The British offensive continues, 10 April–4 May

Having made spectacular gains across the British front on 9 April, General Haig ordered further division- and corps-sized attacks to exploit the German disorder, even if artillery support and intelligence was lacking. Haig had made a commitment to maintain the attack to support the French offensive that was due to begin on 16 April. The BEF had to maintain pressure on the German 6th Army to hold down the enemy reserve forces, thus enabling a breakthrough on the French front when they finally attacked.

On 11 April, the 4th Australian Division attacked with the objective of seizing the village of Bellecourt. The Australian attack, without adequate artillery support as the British were still trying to bring up guns through terrain scarred by the preliminary bombardment, faced the German 27th Division, a veteran unit that had been sent as reinforcements. The Germans had created a coordinated fire plan supported by mobile artillery groups. Effective German artillery fire beat back the attack, the Australians suffering 2,339 casualties. By 11 April, the crisis in the German Supreme High command had passed, and with von Lossberg in place, the Germans were using their elastic defence properly and preparing large counter-attacks.

## Arras Front, 11 April–4 May

The British commanders in the Arras sector now faced a new situation. While the reconnaissance and artillery support plan had worked to perfection on 9 April, they now had to plan and execute large-scale attacks with little time to prepare or conduct detailed reconnaissance. For the next three weeks, the British and the Germans would mount a series of large-scale corps attacks, which would all require extensive aerial reconnaissance and artillery spotting to work. The Arras sector thus saw the heaviest air combat yet seen on the Western Front.

The primary goal for both the British and the German fighter forces was to enable their own observation and artillery planes to do their work, while hindering the enemy's operations. The British sent up their observation and artillery aircraft, mostly B.E.2s but also some new R.E.8s, with heavy fighter escorts. Two-thirds of the RFC fighters were detailed to operate on the front lines, with the remainder conducting patrols deep behind the German lines.

Like the British, the German corps observation and artillery flights were the main focus of their air effort, managed by the air group commanders assigned to each corps. German corps support aircraft were escorted by the Schustas. Meanwhile, German Jastas were detailed to engage British aircraft that crossed deep behind German lines within their respective zones. Because a great part of the British effort was now focused on the Douai Plain, close to Jasta 11's airfield, Manfred von Richthofen's fighter unit was in constant action.

The British mounted major attacks on 13 April. In the meantime, the German 6th Army was reinforced with new divisions. The 6th Army aviation force also received reinforcements. On 9 April, the 6th Army had six fighter squadrons, each officially assigned 12 aircraft, but normally only seven or eight aircraft were serviceable due to many being repaired or overhauled. In the opening attack, the Germans actually had no more than 40-odd fighter planes to oppose the British. But by 12 April, two new fighter squadrons had reinforced the 6th Army, and on 1 May, in anticipation of the final major British offensive, two more fighter squadrons were added. Thus, during intense air combat in April, the German 6th Army had about 50 serviceable fighters, this number rising to 70 on 1 May. Given the low daily losses of the 6th Army aviation force, German airpower actually increased during the campaign. The 6th Army's reconnaissance/artillery flights were also reinforced after the start of the battle, with six artillery flights added and three additional Schustas transferred from other armies. The ability of the Germans to rapidly reinforce their air units meant that the British squadrons, which had already taken heavy losses during the preparatory weeks of the attack, now faced increasing numbers of German aircraft as well as additional flak guns. German flak units would shoot down 75 aircraft on the Western Front in April 1917.

On 15 April, the Germans launched a corps attack on the British 3rd Army, which had now brought up its artillery. British corps artillery flyers accurately targeted the German build-up and attack, which was readily beaten back with heavy casualties. The next major attack by the British was on 23 April, when nine divisions attacked the heavily fortified town of Rouex. German artillery was quite effective that day, the British suffering 10,000 casualties for minimal gains.

General Haig met with General Nivelle near Amiens on 24 April, when Nivelle assured Haig that the French attack at Chemin des Dames – though

Captain Albert Ball joined the Royal Flying Corps at the age of 18, just after the start of the war, becoming a pilot in 1915. He had an impressive flying career, bringing down 44 enemy aircraft before his death in a crash towards the end of the Arras Campaign. After joining No. 56 Squadron, he made several modifications to his own S.E.5, which were later adopted for the definitive S.E.5a mass-production model. When he died aged 21, he was the most famous ace in the RFC. (The Print Collector/ Getty Images)

# Arras

**1** March 1917. RFC conducts extensive reconnaissance of German 6th Army front to identify defences and artillery positions. Extensive aerial mapping (not numbered on diagram).

**2** March 1917. By mid-March the Luftstreitkräfte's long range reconnaissance identified the massive British logistics build-up in the Arras sector, the arrival of new divisions and increase in RFC units (not numbered on diagram).

**3** March 1917. The RFC strongly reinforces the 1st, 3rd and 5th RFC Brigades with each wing receiving two–three more squadrons (not numbered on diagram). Half of the combat power of the RFC is committed to the Arras front.

**4** 15 March–9 April. German Supreme High Command commits nine additional divisions to reinforce the 6th Army in the Arras sector. Luftstreitkräfte's headquarters pulls reconnaissance and artillery flights from other armies plus Jastas to reinforce the 6th Army.

BETHUNE

LENS

ARRAS

9

9

9

4

9

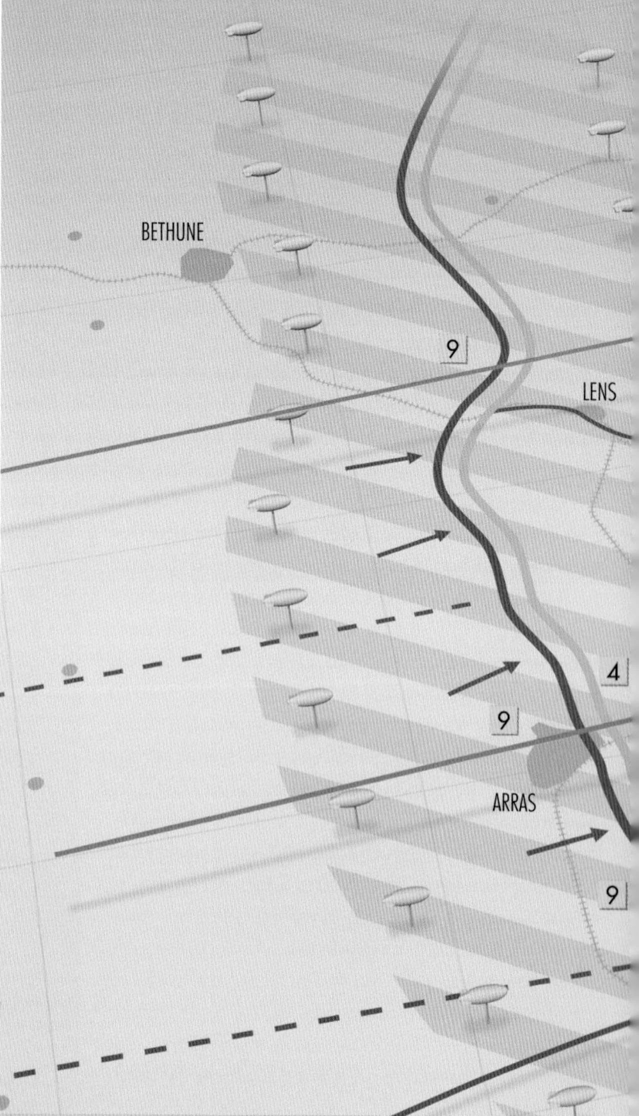

## EVENTS

**5** 1–8 April. German Jastas attack British observation balloons located 10km behind the front lines (not numbered on diagram).

**6** 1–8 April. RFC fighter squadrons attack German observation balloons. Aerial reconnaissance increased. Between 5–7 April RFC observers take 1,700 aerial photos of German defences. RFC artillery pilots active over the front when British preparatory bombardment begins on 5 April. Around the front lines Jastas seek out British artillery flyers. The RFC takes heavy losses

even before the offensive begins (not numbered on diagram).

**7** 5 April. RFC commits one third of its fighters on the Arras front to long-range sweeps in squadron strength deep behind the German lines to engage the Jastas and escort long-range reconnaissance. RFC units fly up to 90km behind German lines at 10,000ft–15,000ft. Heavy losses for the RFC. RFC's fighter sweeps continue until the 4 May.

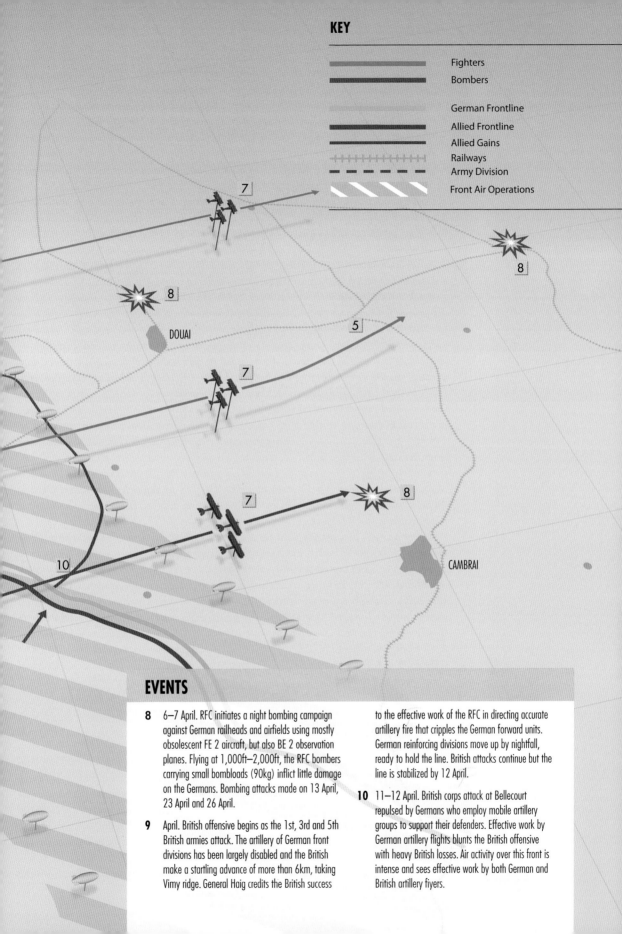

## KEY

- Fighters
- Bombers
- German Frontline
- Allied Frontline
- Allied Gains
- Railways
- Army Division
- Front Air Operations

7

8

8

DOUAI

5

7

7

8

10

CAMBRAI

## EVENTS

**8** 6–7 April. RFC initiates a night bombing campaign against German railheads and airfields using mostly obsolescent FE 2 aircraft, but also BE 2 observation planes. Flying at 1,000ft–2,000ft, the RFC bombers carrying small bombloads (90kg) inflict little damage on the Germans. Bombing attacks made on 13 April, 23 April and 26 April.

**9** April. British offensive begins as the 1st, 3rd and 5th British armies attack. The artillery of German front divisions has been largely disabled and the British make a startling advance of more than 6km, taking Vimy ridge. General Haig credits the British success to the effective work of the RFC in directing accurate artillery fire that cripples the German forward units. German reinforcing divisions move up by nightfall, ready to hold the line. British attacks continue but the line is stabilized by 12 April.

**10** 11–12 April. British corps attack at Bellecourt repulsed by Germans who employ mobile artillery groups to support their defenders. Effective work by German artillery flights blunts the British offensive with heavy British losses. Air activity over this front is intense and sees effective work by both German and British artillery flyers.

bogged down badly – would continue, so the British needed to maintain the offensive. Consequently, the British 3rd Army attacked with four divisions on 28 April, but the assault went badly. Fog and overcast conditions hindered RFC reconnaissance efforts, which failed to spot strong German counter-attack forces moving into position. After the failure of 28 April, 3rd Army commander General Edmund Allenby was determined to carry out a breakthrough attack with 14 divisions on 4 May.

In that attack, the British gained some ground and took several heavily fortified villages. Though the British counter-battery effort had improved, the Germans had deployed enough artillery, well served by German air observers, to stop any breakthrough. The British attack on 4 May effectively ended the campaign, although the British Army would continue to mount divisional and corps attacks in the Arras sector throughout that month.

General Trenchard's fears of going into the spring battles of 1917 with mostly obsolescent aircraft were realized in the massive casualties suffered by the RFC during April, losses so heavy that it was given the name 'Bloody April'. The one bright spot for the RFC was the deployment of No. 56 Squadron, equipped with the new S.E.5s, on the Arras front in the last week of April. Unlike most of the British squadrons, which had been reorganized for specialist functions during the Somme Campaign, No. 56 Squadron had been specifically created as a new unit in late 1916 to fly the S.E.5, which had first flown only in the autumn of that year. The commander of No. 56 Squadron was given full leeway to recruit his own pilots to fly the new airplane, much like the experienced pilots carefully recruited to man the first German Jastas in that autumn. No. 56 Squadron was composed of experienced pilots and included one of Britain's top aces, Captain Albert Ball, who had proven to be a deadly sharpshooter flying the Nieuport scouts. In short, No. 56 Squadron was created from the start as an elite unit and was now to fly Britain's first fighter equipped with two forward-firing machine guns. Nevertheless, some of the British pilots of No. 56 Squadron were sceptical of the S.E.5. Captain Ball even received special permission from General Trenchard himself to continue to fly his own Nieuport fighter while on operations for the squadron.

However, their first patrols with the S.E.5 turned Ball and the other pilots into true believers in this plane, which was considerably faster than the Albatros and fully equal in firepower. The S.E.5's speed advantage allowed it to take the initiative either to start or break off combat. The S.E.5's superior performance was also an advantage at higher altitudes, to where fighter combat was now progressing. Due to the better performance of the S.E.5 above 10,000ft, it was far superior to the Nieuports that comprised a large part of the British fighter forces. The impressive performance of the S.E.5 in late April and early May on the Arras front encouraged the RFC to make certain modifications to the aircraft suggested by Captain Ball, resulting in the S.E.5a. Equipped with a larger 180hp engine, the S.E.5a had a top speed of 125mph.

## Battle on the Chemin des Dames Front
### Advance warning of the French attack

In addition to German reconnaissance reports of an Allied troop and logistics build-up and increased air activity along narrow sectors of the front, the Germans had an additional stroke of luck to inform them of Allied preparations for the attack. During a routine trench raid on 4 April, troops of the German 7th Army captured a French sergeant carrying an entire French corps attack plan. Not only did the captured document provide the schedule, phases, unit objectives and artillery targets for that entire corps, but it also provided a summary of the attack schedule for the units and artillery targets of the two adjacent corps. It was an incredible breach of security to entrust an NCO or officer on the front lines with the complete attack plan. Despite learning of this breach of security, General Nivelle decided to ignore it owing to his faith that, whatever happened, his massive artillery bombardment would simply crush the German defences and allow his forces to walk through the enemy lines with minimal casualties. So, despite handing the Germans their plans, the French made no effort to alter their attack.

### Chemin des Dames attack, 16–18 April

As the battle opened on the Chemin des Dames front on 16 April, the French observation and artillery pilots, despite heavy losses, had done their job well. French artillery pilots had been a constant presence over the German front, even in very marginal weather. French observers were able to take thousands of photographs and monitor German movements. Thanks to the French artillery flyers, German counter-battery fire prior to the attack on the 16th was minimal. The German heavy batteries withheld their fire, knowing that their gun flashes would be spotted by the French artillery flyers, and the French heavy guns – which far outnumbered those of the Germans – would then bring heavy suppressive fire.

The German divisions in the first defence line had suffered heavy casualties during the nine days of preliminary bombardment. Moreover, the commanders at the front reported that their defences had in many places been obliterated by the accurate French shelling. Yet the German defence in depth had only been damaged, not paralyzed, and the German 7th and 1st Army commanders had employed the new doctrine of elastic defence and thus had reserves and reinforcing divisions, with supporting mobile artillery groups, in position to defend or counter-attack.

For the French Army, 16 April was one of the darkest days of the war. Despite as many as 200,000 French infantry of the first wave going over the top to assault the German lines, in many sectors the attack was stopped cold. By 0900hrs, the French 10th Division alone had lost over 5,000 men, while the 15th Division had been unable to advance beyond its own trenches. In other sectors, the decimated German front-line divisions put up a fierce fight before withdrawing to the main defensive line. The primary opponent of the French Army and Air Service on the day of the attack remained the weather. The French plan called for contact patrols to monitor the advance and report the ground situation to the army commanders. However, fog and overcast conditions across the entire region inhibited these patrols, and two aircraft were actually lost in the overcast, landing at German airfields by mistake. French contact patrols were thus unable to give the army commanders a clear picture of the ground situation, the poor visibility making it difficult to spot the signal panels laid out by the infantry units, while signal flares went unnoticed amidst the ongoing artillery fire. As a result, throughout the day, French senior commanders had little idea of what was happening on the ground.

# An inauspicious start for a great combat aircraft

On 5 April 1917, the first air combat took place between the Bristol F.2A and the Albatros D.III. That morning, the new Bristol two-seat fighter made its first combat patrol, despite clouds and fog. By late morning, visibility had improved and a flight of six Bristols from No. 48 Squadron, led by Captain William Robinson VC, encountered a flight of five Albatros D.IIIs from Jasta 11, led by Oberleutnant Manfred von Richthofen (he was promoted to Rittmeister two days later).

Robinson, who had won the Victoria Cross for shooting down a Zeppelin in 1916, had little experience in fighting the German Jastas. Encountering the Germans over Douai, Robinson took a cautious approach and bunched his aircraft together in a tight formation before heading home – hoping that the mutual defensive fire of the rear gunner/observers would drive the Germans away. The British pilots flew their machines as if they were the staid B.E.2s rather than the well-powered, highly maneuverable aircraft that they were. It was a fatal mistake, as the speedy and rugged Bristols would later prove themselves excellent in a dogfight. Diving on the British formation, von Richthofen shot down two of the Bristols, Leutnant Simon another and Vizefeldwebel Festner a fourth – that of Captain Robinson. Only two Bristols returned to base, with one so badly damaged that it had to be scrapped. The Jasta 11 flight suffered no damage.

Captain Joseph Vuillemin (r), commander of the C 11 Observation Squadron in 1917. One of France's star artillery fliers, Vuillemin was a pre-war artillery officer who became a pilot before the war. Vuillemin flew hundreds of hours in the Verdun and Somme Campaigns and flew over the Chemin des Dames. A skilled and aggressive pilot, he liked to take on German observation aircraft. He and his observer were credited with seven air victories by the end of the war. He was awarded the Légion d'honneur for his aerial exploits. In 1939 and 1940, Vuillemin served as Chief of Staff of the French Air Force. (AC)

General Nivelle had placed great hopes in the tanks as a means to break through the German defences. However, the first French tank attack of the war carried out by 128 Schneider and St Chamond tanks in the French 5th Army sector was a disaster. German 7th Army commander General von Boehn was aware that the British had used tanks on the Somme the previous summer, so he ordered the first line of trenches to be widened to create a tank trap. The French tank advance was spotted by German observation planes and the defenders given warning. The Germans had a strong counter-attack force waiting, and the German front and mobile artillery groups were ready. Many tanks broke down, others being caught in the first trench, and 57 more were destroyed by German artillery. At the end of the first day, only 11 tanks were still serviceable and little ground had been gained.

Neither did French aviation contribute much to the battle that day. Some French fighters strafed the German front lines, but French artillery flyers were largely unable to make out the situation on the ground and bring artillery fire onto the German reserves. The Germans flew only limited missions on the 16th due to marginal weather. However, some artillery flyers and fighters did get airborne that day, performing some good service for the defenders in targeting the French attackers.

On the French 5th Army front, the battle went badly on 16 April, with only slight advances made for heavy losses. The fight on the French 6th Army front, however, went better, with German first-line troops battered by the preliminary bombardment being pushed back and advances of up to 2km being made. In several sectors, immediate German counter-attacks by the reserve divisions, supported by mobile artillery groups, contained the French. Unlike the real threat of a breakthrough that existed at Arras on 9 April, at the end of that day the German 7th Army commander could report to the Supreme High Command that the situation was in hand.

Although General Nivelle saw only positive news of German prisoners or guns being taken, the mood at the French Army General Headquarters was morose even before the offensive began. Nivelle was so confident in his tactics that he planned for only 10,000 casualties on the first day of the Chemin des Dames offensive. When Nivelle's tactics failed and the German defence produced 40,000 casualties on that first day alone, and massive casualties over the next two weeks, the French forward medical stations and hospitals were overwhelmed.

Captain Georges Guynemer was a top French fighter ace, shown here in his Nieuport 17. Guynemer won fame as a fighter pilot over Verdun in early 1916. By the time of the Chemin des Dames Offensive, he had been promoted to captain. He was killed in September 1917 after 54 aerial victories. Guynemer won the affection of the French media by his daring and stubbornness. He was shot down eight times in combat, each time returning quickly to the battle. (AC)

Many wounded troops suffered and died needlessly because of a lack of planning to provide adequate medical care.

A major offensive was made by the French 4th Army on 17 April against the southern flank of the Chemin des Dames, the German 1st Army sector. The battle went much as the fighting on the previous day, with heavy French and German losses for only incremental gains. German reserves were in place to counter any threat of a breakthrough. The biggest advance that month came on the night of 17–18 April, when the German 7th Army pulled back three divisions from a salient in front of the Malmaison position to secondary positions under the cover of darkness. The French advanced 7km and captured 100 guns that the Germans had been unable to take with them, as well 5,000 POWs. Yet the main German defence line still held firm.

Despite continuing severe weather on 17 April, some German artillery flyers were able to get airborne and support the German counter-attacks launched against the French 5th and 6th armies. The French had their artillery flyers up too, and both sides took heavy casualties from artillery. With only a handful of fighters to cover the front due to Commandant du Peuty's orders to employ French fighters well behind the German lines, the German artillery flyers were relatively unmolested. A French lieutenant-colonel of the 6th Army Colonial Infantry Corps complained that he lost half his battalion on the 17th to accurate artillery fire directed by German planes. The Germans also began to employ their Schustas in ground attacks near the front, with the French 112th Heavy Artillery Regiment being strafed by German aircraft several times that day.

## Chemin des Dames Front, 18 April–4 May

By 20 April, there was a pause in operations as both armies were exhausted and had taken heavy casualties. On 21 April, Nivelle committed the French 10th Army into the attack, allowing the 5th and 6th armies to pull some of their shattered divisions out of the line. The 10th Army, which had been intended to be the pursuing force for routed German formations after the breakthrough, now carried out a series of large-scale attacks. As before, the French took heavy losses for minor gains. For the next week, the French attacked and the Germans counter-attacked, with both sides able to use artillery to sometimes shatter an attack just as it was beginning. Whenever the weather permitted, artillery flyers made the heavy guns

# Chemin des Dames

## EVENTS

**1**  March 1917. The French Air Service carries out extensive reconnaissance in the area of the Chemin des Dames defended by the German 7th and 1st armies. French Army and Air Service carry out massive logistics and troop movements west of the Chemin des Dames front. The French Reserve Army Group is assembled and the French Air Service is reinforced to 800 aircraft.

**2**  March 1917. German air reconnaissance spots the French deployment of forces and the German 7th and 1st armies are strongly reinforced (not numbered on diagram). The Luftstreitkräfte deploys additional observation and artillery flights to the 7th and 1st armies, as well as additional Jastas.

**3**  15 March–31 March. German Jastas attack French observation balloons. During March, 14 French balloons are destroyed or damaged. From 1–15 April, a further ten are damaged (not numbered on diagram).

**4**  6–15 April. The French carry out pre-attack artillery preparation along the entire 40km front at Chemin des Dames including intensive operations by French observation and artillery escadrilles (not numbered on diagram). French artillery fliers take heavy losses, but still enable the French artillery to devastate the German front line and inflict heavy losses.

**5**  5–7 April. French fighter groups begin long-range sweeps of 15–20 fighters as deep as 90km behind the German front lines — usually at 10,000ft–15,000ft– to draw German Jastas into combat. The Jastas refuse to contest, and are deployed against French artillery and observation aircraft on the front lines. The French conduct large fighter sweeps behind German lines throughout April.

## KEY

| | |
|---|---|
| ▬▬▬▬▬ | Fighters |
| ▬▬▬▬▬ | Bombers |
| | |
| ▬▬▬▬▬ | German Frontline |
| ▬▬▬▬▬ | Allied Frontline |
| ▬▬▬▬▬ | Allied Gains |
| ┼┼┼┼┼┼┼┼┼┼ | Railways |
| ▬ ▬ ▬ ▬ | Army Division |
| ▰ ▰ ▰ ▰ | Front Air Operations |
| ➜ | Allied Attacks |

onne

Juvincourt

Rheims

## EVENTS

**6** 13–14 April. Three escadrilles of French Paul Schmitt bombers – an obsolete two-seater single engine bomber with a top speed of 84mph and a bombload of 90kg – carry out low level (1000ft–2000ft) bombing raids on the German railheads of Marle and Crécy-sur-Serre east of Laon. French bombers inflict minimal damage.

**7** 16 April. The French offensive begins as 200,000 troops of the 5th and 6th armies try to break through the battered German lines. Some divisions are stopped by German defences but in several places the French make small gains, however they fail to break through the main German defence line. French casualties are heavy. Despite bad weather the French observation and artillery aircraft are flying. However, due to low clouds and overcast skies, French artillery flyers often cannot identify the units or situation on the ground and cannot effectively direct artillery fire.

**8** 17–18 April. The Germans evacuate two divisions from a salient in front of Ft. Malmaison on the northern part of the Chemin des Dames front. The French advance 4km and take 5,000 German prisoners and 100 German guns, but Ft. Malmaison and the main German defence line holds.

**9** 17 April. The French 4th Army attacks the southern end of the Chemin des Dames. The French experience heavy casualties for only moderate gains.

**10** 16–23 April. The most intensive part of the offensive with over 100,000 French casualties in the first week (not numbered on diagram). Air activity from both sides is intense along the front as the Germans conduct corps-sized counter-attacks. Relentless French attacks result in minimal gains. Exhausted divisions of the 5th and 6th armies are withdrawn and the French 10th Army moves into the line and continues the attack for the next week.

**11** 28 April. As French attacks continue with heavy casualties, a company of the 5th Army refuses to go into attack and unit mutinies begin, eventually affecting half the divisions of the French Army as morale collapses (not numbered on diagram). Although French attacks continue into May, the offensive is basically ended by 4 May.

**12** 2 May. French Paul Schmitt light bombers carry out night attacks on German airfields in the German 6th Army sector. The old bombers with small bombloads inflict minimal damage.

especially lethal. By 25 April, the French Army had lost an estimated 134,000 casualties. German losses were lower, but still high. Along the front, air activity was intense whenever the weather permitted flying. It was the weather, not opposition aircraft, which proved the greatest enemy of the air services in April 1917. The high French accident rate in April, with more aircraft and aircrew lost than to combat, can be attributed to trying to fly largely obsolescent aircraft in ice, snow, rain and fog.

## The French Army mutinies

Having been promised the final offensive that would end the war, the morale of the French Army on the Chemin des Dames front collapsed in the bloody and indecisive fighting that followed. On 29 April, a company of the 20th Division refused to go back into the front line. Mutinies, usually a unit refusing to attack or go into the line, referred to officially as 'collective indiscipline', began with small units and then larger ones, and then became rampant throughout the French Army during May and June 1917. Most French Army divisions – 68 out of 112 – were affected by incidents of mass indiscipline. There were even armed confrontations between mutinous and loyal troops. In the meantime, Nivelle continued his offensive with a series of corps-sized attacks going into early May. The French government, seeing that the campaign had failed, pressured Nivelle to stop the offensive, before dismissing him on 17 May and appointing General Philippe Pétain in his place as Army Chief of Staff.

Pétain took immediate action to quell the mutinies and raise morale. He established a regular leave policy for front-line soldiers, improved the food and conditions of the rear camps and travelled to every army division to listen to the troops. He promised them there would be no more offensives such as that launched by Nivelle, and that when the French Army fought it would have materiel superiority. The government and military kept the mutinies secret, and clandestine military courts-martial tried ringleaders of mutinous units. A total of 412 death sentences were imposed, but only 57 men were executed, with the other mutineers sent to carry out hard labour in North Africa where they could not tell their story.

The French Army mutiny of 1917 faded out in a few weeks thanks to General Pétain's reforms. At the same time as he addressed the morale problems, Pétain looked to learn the lessons from the failed Nivelle Offensive and initiated major changes to French ground and air doctrine.

## Losses and lessons for the air campaigns of April 1917

The Nivelle Offensive never stood a chance of success. The Germans spotted the build-up weeks before the attack began and thus had time to improve defences and reinforce the threatened sectors. Operation *Alberich* was a success, ensuring the German Army had enough general reserve divisions to counter the Allied attacks. The German defensive strategy proved itself quite effective.

It was a bloody campaign for both sides. Except for a few instances, such as the attack at Arras and Vimy Ridge on 9 April, both defenders and attackers had been able to deploy ample artillery to break up attacks and counter-attacks. Attacks might succeed in gaining some ground, but usually at a prohibitive cost in casualties.

In the 25 days of battle on the Arras front (between 9 April and 4 May), the three British armies in the campaign suffered 158,660 casualties, the highest daily death rate for the British Army for the entire war. The record of German 6th Army casualties is incomplete, but a good general estimate is that the Germans in the Arras sector took 120,000 casualties. Of those, one has to include 20,859 German soldiers captured by

The Luftstreitkräfte deployed searchlight units along with the flak forces for the defence of German airfields and rear installations. (AC)

the British. In the Arras sector, the Germans lost 254 guns captured by the British. It is noteworthy that the most German guns overrun and captured by the British came from the first day of the attack, when more than 120 guns were lost in the Vimy Ridge sector alone.

On the Chemin des Dames front, the French Army had an estimated 187,000 casualties in April and May 1917, with 130,000 casualties just in the first week of the attack (16–23 April). The German 7th and 1st armies lost an estimated 163,000 men in that period. As the battle ended, both the German and British army commanders praised the artillery flyers for their successful direction of the artillery in defence and attack. The artillery flyers played a central role in making 'Bloody April' a bloodbath on the ground for both sides. BEF commander General Haig, in a report to the War Office on 18 May, gave credit to the RFC observation and artillery flyers for their work in making the attacks at Vimy Ridge and in other sectors possible.

On the French and British fronts, the artillery flyers had been effective on the days that the weather cooperated, but their work came at a high price. Of the 178 RFC aircraft lost to combat in the Arras sector during April 1917, most were the two-seater corps aircraft, with 99 shot down, 75 of them being obsolete B.E.2s. During April on the Chemin des Dames front, the French Air Service lost 88 aircraft in combat: 30 fighters and 58 artillery and observation planes. Of the French artillery flyers, 32 of the losses were obsolescent Caudron G.4s, ten of these being shot down on one day, 8 April.

The German losses in combat had been relatively light. At least 76 German aircraft were lost in battle, although records are incomplete and do not include accident losses, which were always high. On the Arras front, the German 6th Army Aviation lost 13 artillery and observation planes and three Shusta aircraft to combat. On the Chemin des Dames front, the German 1st and 7th army aviation lost 11 artillery and observation planes and eight Shusta aircraft. The rest of the German losses during the Nivelle Offensive were Jasta fighters.

There were some harsh lessons learned by the British and French in the air campaign. The tactic of winning air superiority by large fighter patrols deep into enemy territory had failed badly for both the British and French. On the Arras front, the Germans met the RFC's challenge with superior aircraft. On the Chemin des Dames front, the German air

Manfred von Richthofen (centre) and some of the Jasta 11 aces in March 1917. L–R: Vizefeldwebel Festner, Leutnant Schäffer, Leutnant Lothar von Richthofen, Leutnant Wolff. (IWM Q 42284)

commanders wisely refused to confront the French fighters, and instead put the Jastas to work attacking the French artillery and observation aircraft. Despite an almost two-to-one advantage in aircraft numbers, the French Air Service and RFC could not control the airspace over the front lines and deter the German artillery flyers from their mission.

The German organization and communications system had worked effectively to warn the Jastas of enemy activity. The Jastas were outnumbered almost two-to-one in terms of aircraft, but when the weather allowed, they flew three or four missions a day. German aircraft were generally better than those of the British and French air services, although the arrival in combat of the S.E.5 and Sopwith Triplane made the Germans nervous. It was the disparity in training that made the most difference on the Arras front. German pilots were far better trained than their RFC counterparts. From the moment Manfred von Richthofen took command of Jasta 11 in January 1917, he had constantly trained and mentored his pilots. Like other Jasta commanders, he had also recruited new pilots from the ranks of experienced observation and artillery pilots. With trained pilots and good tactics, Jasta 11 scored an astounding 89 aerial victories in April 1917. Furthermore, the Luftstreitkräfte's flak force, larger and more capable than the Allied anti-aircraft units, proved its worth by shooting down 75 Allied aircraft in April.

The air operations of spring 1917 forced many significant changes to the air war. Despite German success in the air during spring 1917, they knew they had to make many changes if they were to stay ahead in the air war. The RFC and French Air Service understood very well that they had too many obsolete planes and that their tactics were deficient. The spring campaign prompted both the RFC and Service Aéronautique to undertake major and immediate changes to their tactics, organization and equipment.

# AFTERMATH AND ANALYSIS

## Air forces adapt after the spring 1917 campaign

The RFC's next campaign after Arras began only a month later in Flanders, which began with the attack on the Messines Ridge on 7 June and continued with the offensive at Ypres from July to October. It was a very different Royal Flying Corps that now engaged the Luftstreitkräfte. Trenchard had fought the Arras Campaign with mostly obsolete aircraft. But now British industry was able to produce up-to-date aircraft in large numbers and RFC squadrons were rapidly re-equipped.

The Sopwith Camel, highly manoeuvrable and equipped with two synchronized machine guns, arrived in June. During the summer, Nieuport squadrons were re-equipped with Camels and the updated S.E.5a, with a larger engine and even faster than the SE.5. The F.2A Bristols, whose capabilities as a fighter were now being exploited by RFC pilots, were slowly appearing at the front. The DH.4 assumed the light bomber role and the main corps aircraft became the R.E.8. By July, 37 of 51 RFC squadrons in France (the others were RNAS) were flying new high-performance aircraft.

The RFC also changed its tactics. While still maintaining its policy of the offensive, more effort was taken to protect the corps artillery planes over the front and to drive away the German artillery planes. In the Flanders Campaign, the RFC set up signals-intercept detachments to monitor German radio transmission bands used by the artillery flyers. Signals stations would get a directional fix on German transmissions and call the information to RFC fighter squadrons, which had a flight of aircraft ready for immediate take-off to intercept and drive away the German artillery flyers. This rapid-response system replaced the inefficient standing fighter patrols which had previously failed to protect RFC corps aircraft and deter German observers.

During the 7 June attack, the RFC put 29 artillery planes over the front and lost only two to German fighters. British aircraft directed fire on 157 German targets that day and British artillery dominated the battlefield. For the next weeks, the British were able to effectively protect their corps flyers.

The SPAD XIII, a derivative of the SPAD VII, arrived at the front in early 1918. Thousands were produced and they eventually equipped almost every French and American fighter squadron. Its 200hp engine gave it a top speed of 130mph and it had excellent flying characteristics. It was armed with two synchronized machine guns. It was one of the top fighters of the war. (IWM Q 66747)

The Sopwith Camel appeared in RFC fighter squadrons in June 1917. Its 130hp rotary engine gave it a top speed of 113 mph. It carried two machine guns and was highly manoeuvrable, but also difficult to fly. It equipped many of the RFC and RAF fighter squadrons. As its performance above 10,000ft was mediocre, it was used extensively in the ground attack role. (Alamy)

## Changes in the Service Aéronautique

Along with practical measures to rebuild French Army morale, General Pétain initiated major reforms in French Army doctrine after evaluating the Nivelle Offensive. Pétain noted that cooperation between the air units and ground forces was deficient. Now, when divisions came out of the line to rest, they were to engage in a two-week intensive training programme that emphasized new weapons and tactics. More attention was paid to teaching the use of ground signals for the airmen, and more training was given to the artillery pilots and artillery headquarters. Pétain ended the doctrine of employing fighters deep behind the lines and ordered fighters instead to operate close to the front to protect French reconnaissance and artillery pilots.

In April 1917, the French Air Service was obsolescent. Pétain's new air commander, Colonel Duval, developed a plan to have more than 2,800 combat aircraft on the Western Front by early 1918, and the French aircraft industry was able to meet these requirements. In the meantime, the Service Aéronautique expanded and improved. The fighter force and observation force were quickly re-equipped. By August, the main aircraft of the fighter force was the SPAD VII. In the artillery/observation escadrilles, obsolete Farmans and Caudrons were scrapped or sent to the training schools, and 302 Caudron G.6s, a twin engine bomber/observer with more powerful engines and greater performance than the G.4, had arrived as replacements. Front units were now equipped with 697 Sopwith 1½ Strutters. Although obsolescent, they were still an improvement over the Farmans and Caudrons. Notably, 32 Salmson 2A single-engine two-seater reconnaissance planes had arrived at front units. With its 270hp engine, the Salmson was fast, manoeuvrable and performed well at high altitudes. It soon became the main aircraft of the French, and later American, reconnaissance units. The Salmson is regarded as one of the best reconnaissance planes of World War I.

The French bomber force saw the arrival of 27 Bréguet 14 bombers in combat units in August. The French aircraft industry produced thousands of the Bréguet 14, which, with its large engine, high speed, performance and 355 kg bombload, revitalized the French bomber force.

In autumn 1917, the final evolution of the Nieuport fighter, the Nieuport 28, appeared. While the Nieuport 17s had been inferior to the Albatros fighters, the Nieuport 28 was faster, but more importantly was armed with two synchronized Vickers machine guns so it could fight the German Albatros D.V on equal terms. It was only a temporary measure, as production of the SPAD XIII was underway, and the SPAD became the main Allied fighter plane of 1918. The SPAD XIII had an improved 220hp Hispano-Suiza engine, a maximum speed of 130mph and was armed with two synchronized Vickers machine guns. It was consequently a match for any German fighter.

# New German doctrine

After the Nivelle Offensive, the Germans changed their tactical organization and doctrine. In June 1917, the Luftstreitkräfte combined four Jastas to form a fighter wing (Jagdgeschwader 1, JG 1), with Rittmeister Manfred von Richthofen as commander. Most of the Jastas were soon organized into wings of four squadrons, each wing commander having a staff to coordinate operations. Large-scale aerial combat, with two or three squadrons operating together, became the norm for air operations. Field army air commanders now had two or more fighter wings under their command, with each wing given an operational sector of the front.

The performance of the Schustas in the spring campaign had impressed the Luftstreitkräfte General Staff. On several occasions on the Arras and Chemin des Dames fronts, they had been used to attack ground troops. In June, the Schustas were renamed *Schlachtstaffel* (battle squadrons, nicknamed 'Schlasta') and given the role of carrying out low-level ground-attack missions. The Schlastas were organized into Schlachtgruppen (battle groups), with three six-plane squadrons. These formations were trained to fly in mass attacks, to support army attacks by targeting the front and immediate rear, with troops and artillery being the prime targets. In the defensive role, the Schlastas would be thrown in to disrupt enemy attacks.

Summer 1917 saw the introduction of the new Hannover CL.III and Halberstadt CL.II two-seater attack planes to equip the Schlastas. These had 5mm armour around the engine, pilot and observer to protect them from ground fire. They were also routinely equipped with 50kg of light bombs. In the Flanders Campaign, the Schlachtgruppen proved their worth on several occasions by disrupting British attacks. The new Luftstreitkräfte operational doctrine published in May 1917 specified that Schlastas would serve as close air support to German divisions in the attack. The attack groups became a major branch of the Luftstreitkräfte, constituting more than 10 per cent of the combat aircraft by early 1918.

The Germans had noted the Allied bombing campaign against airfields and logistics, but before summer 1917 the Luftstreitkräfte had rarely carried out such attacks. Now Germany had a heavy bomber force concentrated in Flanders to attack England with the Gotha G.IV heavy bombers, capable of carrying a 500kg bombload. In the summer campaign over Flanders, the Germans diverted bomber squadrons to attack Allied airfields, rail centres and the ports where the BEF received its supplies. Interdiction bombing now became a major mission for the German bombing force. Using bombers in night attacks required

The Hispano-Suiza eight-cylinder aircraft engine. This engine was a revolutionary design developed in 1914 by Marc Birkigt, a Swiss engineer working for the Hispano-Suiza automobile company. It was adopted by the French Air Service in early 1915 and put into mass production. The 150hp engine featured an innovative cast-aluminium engine block with the cylinders emplaced in steel sleeves screwed into the engine block, reducing weight and making cooling more efficient. By 1917, 200hp and 220hp Hispano-Suiza engines were powering Allied aircraft. Manufactured in the thousands, this was a key piece of technology that enabled the Allied air services to prevail. (Photo by Heritage Art/Heritage Images via Getty Images)

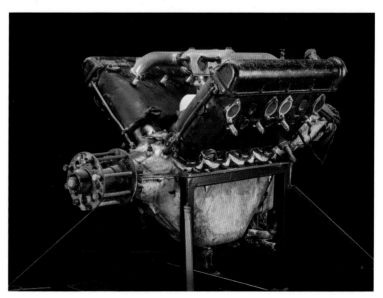

The Hannover CL.II, with a 180hp engine and 103mph top speed, was a sturdy and reliable machine equipping the ground attack units. Many had 5mm of armour fitted to protect the engine and aircrew from ground fire. (AC)

developing new techniques for night navigation, including aerial beacons and special lighting for runways. Despite some successes, the Allied and German bomber campaigns had only a small effect on the movement and supply of munitions and equipment to the front.

## Artillery, airpower and the new way of war

The biggest change for all the armies and air services was the development of new artillery tactics that finally made a breakthrough attack possible without high losses to the attacker. For the Allies, the Spring 1917 Campaign was a signal failure, and the reason was simple: the long build-up period and the days of artillery preparation required for the British and French offensives told the Germans exactly where the Allies would strike long before the attack came. This allowed the Germans to move reserve divisions and mobile artillery groups into place at the threatened sectors. Attacking into prepared reserves, well supported by artillery and ready to counter-attack, made Allied assaults extremely costly in lives.

The answer to restoring the offensive and breaking through defence lines came from two British and German artillery officers, both of whom worked out a solution to the offensive dilemma during experiments in 1917. British Brigadier General Henry Tudor, commander of the BEF's 9th Division's artillery, and German Lieutenant Colonel Georg Bruchmüller, serving as an artillery commander on the Eastern Front, noted that the long artillery preparation time which gave clear warning of any imminent offensive was largely due to the requirement for registering artillery fire. Neither German nor Allied artillery could be accurate unless batteries fired with an observer in a balloon or airplane to adjust the fire onto the target, which was often a laborious process. Once registered, guns could provide highly accurate fire, but the lengthy process of registering hundreds of batteries alerted their opponents to all the sites selected for targeting.

As lifelong artillerymen, both Tudor and Bruchmüller looked for a means to ensure accurate fire without prior registration. First of all, Tudor and Bruchmüller knew that each artillery tube had distinctive characteristics that would affect its accuracy. Both officers mandated that each gun under their command be taken to a firing range behind the lines and test-fired with different elevations and different powder charges, to determine their specific characteristics. The gunners would then develop a firing table for each individual gun. The artillerymen also worked with the military meteorology sections to establish how air temperature and density and wind would affect the fall of projectiles for all the army's different artillery pieces.

These 'slide-rule' artillerymen convinced their respective High Commands that artillery using high-quality maps made from air reconnaissance, and using the new firing and meteorological tables, could achieve reasonably good accuracy without registration fire. They proposed that an attacking army could move up its artillery to already-surveyed gun positions literally on the eve of battle. The army could then attain complete surprise, an attack beginning with a rapid-fire hurricane bombardment, followed by an infantry advance behind artillery covering fire to break through the enemy positions. The idea was to surprise the enemy and gain complete artillery dominance by paralyzing their artillery in the first stage of the attack by drenching it with explosives and gas. Without supporting artillery for the defenders, well-trained attacking infantry with ample fire support could thus break even powerful defence lines with only moderate losses. The success of the concept required thorough aerial photography to identify every enemy artillery battery in the sector to be attacked, so that they could be quickly suppressed with accurate fire and gas shells at the start of the surprise attack.

This new offensive concept was first used on a large scale against the Russian 12th Army in front of Riga, Latvia, on 1 September 1917. The German artillery commanded by Lieutenant Colonel Bruchmüller had been hidden in the Latvian forests behind the lines up to the eve of the German 8th Army's attack with six divisions across the wide Duna (Daugava) River against strongly fortified Russian positions.

There was no registration fire. The attack opened in the early morning with a massive four-hour bombardment of the Russian positions that targeted the defences and every known Russian artillery battery and unit headquarters. German storm troops crossed the river and broke into the Russian defences, with little interference from Russian artillery thanks to German suppressive fire. The Russians, taken completely by surprise, collapsed; by the

German 1917 map of Russian defences in front of Riga on the Eastern Front. Note the detail of fortifications and strongpoints. Buried telephone cables are mapped, and battalion and regimental headquarters are noted and given target numbers. Aerial photography enabled the production of highly detailed maps, which were disseminated down to company level. Accurate maps were essential for employing an army's artillery firepower. (AC)

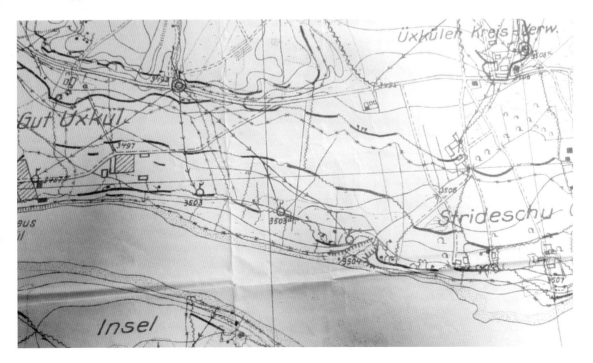

afternoon, all six German divisions had crossed the river and broken into the Russian rear. The Russian 12th Army abandoned 324 guns and retreated, allowing the Germans to take the city of Riga without a battle. At a cost of just 4,000 German casualties, over 20,000 Russian casualties were inflicted. The German victory was a fatal blow to the credibility of the Russian Provisional Government, which collapsed only weeks later, taking Russia out of the war.

## French attack at Malmaison

In October 1917, General Pétain tested the new tactical methods with an attack by seven divisions against the German defences at Malmaison on the German right flank of the Chemin des Dames, a position that the Germans had held against repeated French attacks in April. Without registration fire, the French opened the attack with a massive one-day artillery barrage. Every German strongpoint was targeted by heavy artillery using the new techniques. Two French corps launched their attack behind a creeping barrage employing 1,600 heavy guns. Taken by surprise, German defences fell quickly to the French infantry, while French heavy artillery kept the German regimental and divisional reserves at bay. French air reconnaissance had identified the large dugouts that housed German reserves in the second and third defence lines, and these were specifically targeted, breaking up German counter-attacks before they could form.

The Malmaison operation, as a limited offensive to seize key terrain and consolidate, with a minimum of casualties, lasted only four days, with the French taking Malmaison and advancing several kilometres. The French artillery was especially effective. French losses were 14,000 killed, wounded or missing, while the Germans lost over 25,000 troops, including 12,000 taken prisoner. The French captured 200 German guns and mortars. The French offensive played a key role in restoring the morale of the French Army, which had collapsed during the summer. Not only had the French won a significant battle, but they had done so with half of the casualties of the German defenders who had occupied a strong position.

## British and Germans at Cambrai

The BEF's opportunity to demonstrate the effectiveness of the new methods came on 20 November at Cambrai. The BEF had moved its assault divisions into the line with great secrecy and opened the attack without any preparatory fire, but with a massive barrage directed at German defences and known artillery positions. Behind a wall of covering fire and supported by 300 tanks, the British Army broke into the German lines and pushed the Germans back 10 miles in two days in one of the most dramatic advances of the war. The RFC fighter squadrons massed to control the air and carried out strafing attacks along the German front and rear areas. British casualties were moderate, while the Germans, who had been taken by complete surprise, had some 20,000 men taken prisoner.

After the British had consolidated their gains, the Germans mounted their own surprise counter-attack on 30 November, also without any long preparatory barrage, effectively targeting and suppressing the British artillery with heavy fire as the infantry attacked. In three days, the British were thrown back to their original start lines of 20 November. This time it was the Germans who took 20,000 British prisoners. The Germans concentrated their Jastas to ensure air superiority over the battlefield, and the Schlachtstaffels were used en masse and in direct support of attacking German divisions, bombing and strafing front units and artillery near the front. The Cambrai counter-attack saw the first use of an all-metal armoured biplane, the Junkers J.I, specially designed for ground attack.

These three limited offensives demonstrated to the British, French and Germans that successful breakthrough attacks and the resumption of open warfare without excessive casualties were now possible, thanks to the new artillery doctrine enabled by aerial reconnaissance and detailed planning. The element of surprise returned to the battlefield, and these 1917 battles were the model for battlefield success in the 1918 campaigns.

Although it had been a failure for the Allied attackers and a success for the German defenders, the Spring Campaign of 1917 served as a major catalyst to compel improved tactics and more efficient joint operations in the Allied and German armies. It thus represents a major milestone in the evolution of airpower.

# BIBLIOGRAPHY

Bailey, Frank & Cony, Christophe, *French Air Service War Chronology 1914–1918*, Grub Street, London (2001)

Baring, Maurice, *Flying Corps Headquarters 1914–1918*, Bell and Sons, London (1920)

Christienne, Charles & Lissarague, Pierre, *A History of French Military Aviation*, Smithsonian, Washington DC (1986)

Cochet, Francois & Port, Remy, *Histoire de L'Armee Francais 1914–1918* , Tallandier, Paris (2013)

Corum, James, 'World War I Aviation: From reconnaissance to the modern air campaign', Chapter 4 in *The World War I Companion* (ed. Mathias Strohn), Osprey Publishing, Oxford (2013)

Corum, James S., 'The Air Campaign of 1918' in *1918: Winning the War, Losing the War* (ed. Mathias Strohn), Osprey Publishing, Oxford (2018)

Corum, James S., 'The Old Eagle as Phoenix: The Luftstreitkräfte Creates an Operational Air Doctrine' in *Air Power History* (Spring 1992)

Doughty, Robert, *Pyrrhic Victory: French Strategy and Operations in the Great War*, Belknap Press, Cambridge (2005)

Duroselle, Jean-Baptiste, *La Grand Guerre des Francais 1914–1918*, Perrin, Paris (1994)

État-Major des Armées, Service Historique, *Les Armées Françaises dans la Grande Guerre*, Tome V, Vol. 1, *L'Offensive d'Avril 1917*, Imprimerie Nationale, Paris (1931–32)

Franks, Norman, Bailey, Frank & Guest, Russell, *Above the Lines*, Grub Street, London (1993)

Franks, Norman, Giblin, Hal & McCrery, Nigel, *Under the Guns of the Red Baron*, Barnes and Noble, New York (1999)

Franks, Norman, Guest, Russell & Bailey, Frank, *Bloody April 1917*, Grub Street, London (2017)

Franks, Norman & Van Wyngarden, Greg, *Fokker Dr 1 Aces of World War I*, Osprey Press, Oxford (2001)

Gray, Peter & Thetford, Owen, *German Aircraft of the First World* War, Putnam, London (1962)

Guttman, Jon, *Reconnaissance and Bomber Aces of World War I*, Osprey, Oxford (2015)

Hallion, Richard, *Rise of the Fighter Aircraft, 1914–1918*, Nautical and Aviation Publishing, Annapolis (1984)

Hart, Peter, *Aces Falling: War above the Trenches, 1918*, Weidenfeld & Nicolson, London (2007)

Hart, Peter, *Bloody April: Slaughter in the Skies over Arras, 1917*, Weidenfeld & Nicolson, London (2005)

Hoeppner, General der Kavallerie Ernst, *Deutschlands Krieg in der Luft*, Koehler und Amelang, Leipzig (1921)

Jones, H. A., *The War in the Air*, Vol. IV, Clarendon Press, Oxford (1934)

Kilduff, Peter, *Germany's First Air Force 1914–1918*, Motorbooks International, Osceola (1991)

Kilduff, Peter, *Richthofen: Beyond the Legend of the Red Baron*, John Wiley and Sons (1993), also Arms & Armour, London (1995)

Kriegsgeschichtlichen Forschungsanstalt des Heeres, *Die militärischen Operationen zu Lande: Der Weltkrieg 1914 bis 1918*, volume 12, *Die Kriegsführung im Frühjahr 1917*, E. S. Mittler Verlag, Berlin (1925–30)

Kriegswissenschaftlichen Abteilung der Luftwaffe, *Entwicklung und Einsatz der deutschen Flakwaffe und des Luftschutzes im Weltkrieg*, E. S. Mittler, Berlin (1938)

Levine, Joshua, *Fighter Heroes of WWI*, Collins, London (2008)

Lewis, Cecil, *Sagittarius Rising*, Greenhill Books, London (1993, originally published in 1936 by Peter Davies Ltd)

Lloyd, Nick, *Western Front: A History of the Great War, 1914–1918*, W. W. Norton & Co., New York (2021)

Miller, Russell, *Boom: The Life of Viscount Trenchard, Father of the Royal Air Force*, Weidenfeld & Nicolson, London (2016)

Morrow, John, *German Air Power in World War I*, University of Nebraska Press, Lincoln (1982)

Morrow, John, *The Great War in the Air*, Smithsonian, Washington (1993)

Murphy, David, *Breaking Point of the French Army: The Nivelle Offensive of 1917*, Pen & Sword, Barnsley (2015)

Neumann, Georg, *Die deutschen Luststreitkräfte im Weltkriege*, E. S. Mittler, Berlin (1920)

Nowarra, H. J. & Brown, Kimbough, *Von Richthofen and the Flying Circus*, Harleyford Publications, Letchworth (1958)

Philpott, Brian, *Encyclopedia of German Military Aircraft*, Bison Books, London (1981)

Revell, Alex, *No 56 Sqn RAF/RFC*, Osprey, Oxford (2009)

Routledge, Brigadier N. W., *Anti-Aircraft Artillery 1914–55*, Brassey's, London (1994)

Sheldon, Jack, *The German Army in the Spring Offensives 1917: Arras, Aisne & Champagne*, Pen & Sword, Barnsley (2015)

Shores, Christopher, Franks, Norman & Guest, Russell, *Above the Trenches*, Grub Street, London (1990)

Slessor, John, *The Central Blue: The Autobiography of Sir John Slessor, Marshal of the RAF*, Praeger, New York (1957)

Sumner, Ian, *Kings of the Air: French Aces and Airmen of the Great War*, Pen & Sword Military, Barnsley (2015)

Sumner, Ian & Sumner, Graham, *German Air Forces 1914–18*, Osprey, Oxford (2005).

Treadwell, Terry & Wood, Alan, *German Fighter Aces of World War One*, Tempus Publishing, Stroud (2003)

Uffindell, Andrew, *The Nivelle Offensive and the Battle for the Aisne*, Pen & Sword, Barnsley (2015)

Westermann, Edward, *Flak: German Anti-Aircraft Defenses, 1914–1945*, University Press of Kansas, Lawrence (2001)

Williams, George, *Biplanes and Bombsights; British Bombing in World War I*, Air University Press, Maxwell AFB (1999)

Winter, Dennis, *The First of the Few: Fighter Pilots of the First World War*, University of Georgia Press, Athens (1983)

# INDEX